Given in Memory
of

Mary Matakitis

by

Chris and Charlie Carroll

and

Mary Sirimis

2000

Gardens in the City

Gardens in the City

New York in Bloom

Text by **Mary Jane Pool**

Photography by **Betsy Pinover Schiff**

Foreword by **David Rockefeller**

Harry N. Abrams, Inc., Publishers

Contents

Foreword

This book contains dramatic photographs and fascinating details that reveal the diverse and often hidden landscapes of New York City. I am thrilled that it brings to the world's attention many historic gardens as well as many exciting new ones, as I believe gardens add so much to the rich tapestry of a city's life. I am honored that the authors have included a number of gardens associated with my family.

Public horticulture has long been an interest of the Rockefellers. The beauty and serenity of a city garden, and the garden as a setting for cultural and educational activities has led us through the years to be active in developing several. I am happy they contribute to the important role gardens are playing as city populations increase and cityscapes expand.

At the turn of the century my grandfather, John D. Rockefeller, was an advocate and patron of The New York Botanical Garden. The work there continues to benefit mankind, to educate, and to give pleasure to New Yorkers. In the 1930s the formal rooftop and Channel Gardens and the plaza plantings at Rockefeller Center set a new pattern for landscaping an urban complex. The dramatic combination of nature and architecture, the seasonal garden displays, and the spectacular Christmas tree attract millions of visitors to the center city every year.

In 1938 The Cloisters was opened to the public in Frederick Law Olmsted's beautiful Fort Tryon Park. This reconstruction of a medieval monastery from architectural artifacts, and its collection of medieval art and horticulture was a project dear to my father, John D. Rockefeller, Jr. He worked for twenty years to see it to completion. The Cloisters was his gift to The Metropolitan Museum of Art, along with medieval art from his own collection, including the Unicorn Tapestries. Plants depicted in the tapestries appear in the cloister gardens, and these gardens are an ongoing study of plants of the Middle Ages that can contribute to our living today.

In 1953 the Abby Aldrich Rockefeller Sculpture Garden at The Museum of Modern Art was dedicated. This oasis of sculpture in midtown Manhattan was named for my mother, one of the founders of the Museum. It was the first garden in America designed for the exhibition of modern sculpture. At the dedication ceremony Trygvie Lie, first Secretary General of the United Nations, spoke of mother's vision for a museum and sculpture garden promoting international understanding through modern art.

It was my sister Abby Rockefeller Mauzé who conceived Greenacre Park, a small garden of trees, flowering shrubs, and a sculptural waterfall on East 51st Street. At the opening in October, 1971 she expressed her pleasure in making the park available to her fellow New Yorkers, with the hope they would find there some moments of serenity in this busy world. The Park is maintained by her Greenacre Foundation that also sponsors an outreach program including summer work for youths in Manhattan parks, neighborhood tree-plantings, and assistance for park designs and restorations.

My own love of nature and art led me to endorse the 1956 plan of The Rockefeller Institute trustee's for fifteen acres of natural beauty as the setting for the developing university. The great lawn with its allée of London plane trees, the sculpture, and the formal gardens and fountains create an environment conducive to research and study in a crowded city. Rockefeller University is a good example of why such a campus need not be in a rural setting, away from the creative energy of a metropolitan area.

In September of 1988 the Peggy Rockefeller Rose Garden was dedicated at The New York Botanical Garden. This garden honors my wife for her lifetime commitment to horticulture spaces of beauty and tranquility. Peggy served on the Garden's Board of Managers for ten years and played the dominant role in supporting the Garden's publication of the six volume Wildflowers of the United States series. She ran the Abby Aldrich Rockefeller Garden in Seal Harbor, Maine, and was actively involved in the work of the American Farmland Trust and the Maine Coast Heritage Trust. The restoration of this historic rose garden, designed in the 1920s by one of America's preeminent landscape architects, Beatrix Jones Farrand, makes it possible for garden lovers again to enjoy one of the greatest public rose gardens in the nation. There, the history of the rose continues to unfold.

At the opening of The Cloisters my father spoke of beauty as one of the great spiritual and inspirational forces of life, having the power to transform duty into radiant living. He hoped The Cloisters, surrounded by nature at her best, would refresh and gladden all those who thirst for beauty. It is gratifying to know that there is a growing understanding of the importance of gardens in the city, and that this book has been created to show their allure and diversity,

David Rockefeller

Editor: Margaret L. Kaplan

Designer: Carol A. Robson

Maps: Christine Edwards

Library of Congress Cataloging-in-Publication Data

Pool, Mary Jane.
    Gardens in the city: New York in bloom/by Mary Jane Pool;
photographs by Betsy Pinover Schiff; with a foreword by David Rockefeller.
        p.   cm.
    Includes index.
    ISBN 0-8109-4133-3 (hardcover)
    1. Gardens–New York (State)–New York. 2. Gardens–New York
(State)–New York–Pictorial works. I. Title.
SB466.U65N7428   1999
712'.6'097471–dc21   98-40693

Published in 1999 by Harry N. Abrams, Incorporated, New York

Harry N. Abrams, Inc.
100 Fifth Avenue
New York, N.Y. 10011
www.abramsbooks.com

Preceding pages:

Endpapers: Autumn on a rooftop terrace

Page 1, above: Thousands of tiny lights in the garden of the Tavern on the Green restaurant in Central Park. *below:* The Isamu Noguchi Sculpture garden in Long Island City. Pictured, the artist's *To Darkness* (1965–66)

Page 2–3: Edith and Hamilton Kean's terrace, looking toward the East River

Page 4–5: Federal Plaza in downtown Manhattan, designed by landscape architect Martha Schwartz

Page 6–7: To link Kathryn Steinberg's terrace to Central Park, garden designer Halsted Wells mixed green textures in low planters

Page 8: Garden at The Frick Collection

Page 9: Garden at The Rockefeller University

Page 78: PHILIP JOHNSON. The Abby Aldrich Rockefeller Sculpture Garden, The Museum of Modern Art, New York. View from above, looking northeast, showing MIRO: *Moonbird* (1966) and CALDER: *Black Widow,* 1959. Garden design 1964: photographed Autumn 1997. Photograph © Betsy Pinover Schiff, 1997, New York. Courtesy The Museum of Modern Art, New York

Page 79: ELIE NADELMAN. *Man in the Open Air* (c. 1915), as installed in The Abby Aldrich Rockefeller Sculpture Garden, The Museum of Modern Art, New York. Gift of William S. Paley (by exchange). Photograph © Betsy Pinover Schiff, 1997, New York. Courtesy The Museum of Modern Art, New York

The City Garden

Gardens are very much a part of city life, and yet, growing next to or on top of buildings of concrete and steel, they still surprise as they delight. A designed garden brings a special kind of visual pleasure, a certain sense of order, and the refreshment of nature to urban life. The green textures, vivid and tender colors, fascinating combinations of plants with other natural materials give both public and private gardens a vitality and beauty that adds immensely to the enjoyment of city living.

Nature and architecture come together in wonderful ways in the five boroughs of New York City. Gardens are growing on rooftops and in yards, along the avenues and in parks, in five botanical gardens that work to protect the world's natural environment, and in scores of community gardens that enhance their neighborhoods. There are gardens for the arts, gardens at the office, gardens for dining, gardens that are part of history, and gardens of the avant-garde that look to the next century. Each of the more than one hundred examples shown in this volume has its own distinct style and spirit.

In the following pages, some of America's most gifted landscape designers and horticulturists generously share their ideas and techniques for designing and planting city gardens. This book is dedicated to them, and to all the people who sow the seeds that keep New York in bloom.

The Lily Pool Terrace in front of the Steinhardt Conservatory pavilions at the Brooklyn Botanic Garden

Roof Gardens

Gardening on the roof of a townhouse or apartment building has its own special rewards. It might be compared to gardening on a mountainside. Spectacular views of parks, rivers, or the architecture of other buildings can more than compensate for the inconvenience of hauling up plant materials and planters. The joy may come simply from having a terrace to extend living spaces, or experiencing the change of seasons through nature in pots and boxes. Whether the garden is on a second-floor rooftop or the fifty-ninth floor of a skyscraper, the challenges are similar. Trees and shrubs must be able to stand up to weather. They must lend themselves to pruning to control shape and size. Containers, potting mixtures, and what goes into them must adhere to weight restrictions. And, when the garden is up high, maintenance must be kept low. Garden specialists are solving the problems of gardening on rooftops with splendid results.

Living a suburban life in the middle of the city—listening to the birds, smelling the roses—appealed tremendously to the couple who bought this duplex penthouse. The previous owner left behind a variety of mature trees, shrubs, and vines. Roots had been pruned through the years to control and enhance growth, and the plants liked their high-in-the-sky situation.

The new owners have carried on the tradition. They called in garden designer Halsted Wells to work with them, preserving what was there as they developed a garden that encircles the apartment on two floors. Planters were repositioned when necessary according to weight limits calculated by an engineering firm. Proper support is a serious issue with gardens that just happen to be a number of floors off the ground.

Trees include birch, maple, American elm, balsam, poplar, cherry, crab apple, and a grafted apple that produces

Preceding pages: A metal gazebo is the decorative and practical design solution to a narrow strip of terrace.

Two floors, two moods

both Delicious and McIntosh varieties. Junipers, azaleas, wisteria, climbing hydrangea, moonflower vines, and morning glory thrive. The intense green borders of the garden make it melt into the green of Central Park and provide a wonderful backdrop for the plants that bloom seasonally. Rich, red Ludovici terra-cotta tile flooring seemed to call for a flower palette of sun colors— white, yellow, orange, scarlet— that stand out against the green plants and those with burgundy foliage.

There are rose beds and perennial beds. A planting box may contain yarrow, ornamental grass, Montauk daisies, and licorice plant. Another, following the seasons, may flower with tulips, lilies, coral bells, black-eyed Susans, cosmos, and zinnias.

On the upper level there is a charming Japanese-style garden, and like a tea garden in Kyoto, it contains traditional elements—steps of beautiful stones, a bamboo gate and trellising, a stone water basin with a bamboo dipper. The plantings include bamboo, weeping cut-leaf Japanese red maple, and mondo grass, set in stainless steel pans averaging 9 inches in height. To hide elevator housing and roof ducts, and to meet building codes, the walls are aluminum tubing fashioned and painted like bamboo. The stones of the path are lightweight fiberglass carefully shaped and colored to blend with the steps. The real and the artificial work together, providing both practical and beautiful results in this small, serene garden.

Overleaf: Looking across Central Park

The highest rooftop garden

On the top of Trump Tower, fifty-nine stories above Fifth Avenue, there is an astonishing garden. On a clear day, Donald Trump can see the harbor, the rivers, the parks, the skyscrapers on all sides, and far beyond. Landscape architect Thomas Balsley believes it to be the highest roof garden in the world.

The ideal time to establish the framework of a roof garden is when a building is under construction, and this is what Balsley, who designed the waterfall in the atrium and other public garden spaces in the building, suggested. Taking into account weight and wind loads, the structural design, waterproofing, drainage, and lighting for the Trump garden were built into the roof system of the tower. All the woodwork is teak, and the copper lighting fixtures softly spotlight certain plantings. Tree lights glow in the night; candles, lanterns, and moonlight do the rest, creating a romantic mood.

One-fourth of the garden is for herbs, vegetables, and cutting beds. Keeping weight in mind, all are grown in Metro Mix, a lightweight soil mixed with coated vermiculite pellets.

Plantings vary with the seasons, but the colors usually range from white to pink to magenta to purple. Along with a Blue Atlas cedar, some hollies, and a lush bed of ivy, there are 'Autumn Glory' sedum, lavender, seafoam roses, Montauk daisies, butterfly bush, and peonies. The Trump roof garden is a breathtaking example of nature enhancing modern-day architecture.

Overleaf: The "crow's nest" is a raised platform for viewing the immense greenness of Central Park.

The dining area, spacious and sparely planted, is framed with Japanese black pines, a wind-tolerant variety. A decorative planter may contain a mass of marigolds at one time, cascading Peruvian geraniums at another. Kentucky bluegrass carpets the play yard, and an evergreen hedge against a lattice backdrop hides some of the building's mechanical works. Purple-leaf plum, hydrangeas, and an assortment of roses, including the popular 'Betty Prior,' add charm and color to the Trump rooftop garden.

A roof garden of rooms

A spectacular contemporary apartment in an industrial loft seemed to call for a garden in a similar mood. Owner Giorgio De Luca brought in the landscape architecture firm of Edmund Hollander Design, which had created a garden for his house in the Hamptons. The terrace of the large top-floor bedroom surrounded by glass was the challenge. Dividing the space into rooms and creating different levels was the solution. Are you inside? Are you outside? This interaction was the feeling Hollander and his project designer, Julie Altoff, sought to establish.

Following the city code that only 25 percent of materials can be flammable, redwood, which grays nicely as it ages, was chosen for the planters and elevated decking. To continue the architectural interest, lawn panels were planted in shallow 4 x 8-foot boxes recessed into the pattern of precast concrete pavers. Bright sun, strong winds, urban pollutants, and salt air from the nearby Hudson bay affect plant materials in much the same way as the salt winds near the ocean. This helped to determine the plantings, which include river birches, olives, white spruces, junipers, hydrangeas, shrub roses, with crab apples for the birds. The palette is mostly gray-green. Ground covers are cotoneaster and euonymus. Tucked into planters are lavender, Russian sage, catmint, lamb's ears, coneflower, and seasonal herbs. According to Hollander, who says small gardens in the city are worth acres in the country, this garden is an extension of the very creative personality of its owner, who is known for his innovative Dean & Deluca food establishments. It successfully combines the best of city terrace living and dining.

Overleaf: Terrace looking toward the river

Being away most of the summer, the owners of this Park Avenue terrace wanted their roof garden to be green and flowery in spring and autumn, the seasons when they are at home.

and helps to pull all the different surfaces together and give the design continuity.

Everything had to be in containers, so they were important in developing the landscape. Here, boxes of

A green-and-white garden

A decorative balustrade that was already in place became the starting point for garden designer Edwina Von Gal. She built a lattice framework to create the effect of a room. Painted dark green, it provides a decorative background for vines and shrubs

cedar made with a tongue-and-groove construction are used for heavier plantings, such as white birch trees. Where weight was a problem, the following formula was used: planter + light-weight soil + tree + water = 52.5 pounds per cubic foot.

White birches are good terrace trees—with their pearly bark they are attractive all year round and tolerate the wind well.

Plants that like this sunny Eastern exposure include scaevola, oak leaf hydrangea, wisteria, caryopteris, sedum, vibernum, and clematis. Pink and white impatiens and pink geraniums in various stone containers add continual bloom and color.

The fountain was designed to be tall. A lead ram's head, made in England, was mounted on a wooden plaque and raised above the catch basin to give the fountain more presence. To lighten the load, the basin is cleverly lined with Styrofoam covered with a shelf and black beach stones. This allows for only three inches of water, which is recirculated. The splashing water always sounds cool and refreshing. Next to the fountain there is an assortment of herbs in pots: chives, parsley, thyme, rosemary, and tarragon.

Sturdy metal furniture, capable of withstanding strong winds, is covered in a durable outdoor fabric printed with a pattern especially designed for this terrace. The overall effect is deliciously green and white.

A penthouse with glass walls opening to a gloriously green garden on all four sides is a dream way to live

were very mature and did not meet new specifications for weight loads, and the planters that held them had

Trees, shrubs, vines, and bulbs were carefully stored in the building's back courtyard. Timothy DuVal, of Plant

The outdoor life high in the sky

in the city for someone who loves the country.

Shortly after Linn Howard moved into the building, management decided it was time to resurface the roof. The existing plantings

to be removed to make way for new paving blocks. So the whole garden had to be taken apart, and was reassembled only many months later. A challenge, indeed.

Specialists, Inc., created a new plan using lighter platforms and containers and looser, lighter potting mixtures. He created a more open effect with the saved plant materials, and chose new additions for their lacy appearance.

Now, young trees—olive, birch, dogwood, holly, juniper, and pine—are seasonally pruned to maintain a pleasing shape and keep growth under control. Vines are trellised. A white wisteria covers the screened gazebo—a wonderfully useful outdoor room for napping or entertaining. Climbing hydrangeas, roses, Casablanca lilies, and grapes mark the seasons. The fountain splashes and the leaves rustle in the fragrant breeze.

A rooftop lawn

On the Upper West Side of Manhattan an interesting L-shaped roof garden has two large panels of green lawn for centerpieces. The landscape architecture firm of Kelly/Varnell designed the garden for a previous owner, and the present owner retains the spirit of the original plan.

After the apartment building had been reroofed and good drainage established, gravel, 3 to 8 inches deep, was laid down, then covered with filter fabric and 3 to 8 inches of good topsoil. The panels, measuring about 22 x 35 feet, are seeded with a Kentucky bluegrass mixture and aerated regularly.

The plantings allow the terrace to blend into the spectacular backdrop of the Central Park Reservoir. There are purple-leaf plum trees, arborvitae, euonymus, Boston and English ivy, climbing roses, clematis, honeysuckle, and other scented plants. Because of the strong summer sun and winter winds, Brem Hyde of Garden Works, who maintains the garden now, uses the hardiest of planting materials. In summer, the hanging baskets are filled with trailing geraniums, and in autumn, pots of chrysanthemums add brilliant color. The garden is seen here at the change of season.

This duplex penthouse, located downtown on Abingdon Square, has spectacular views of Wall Street and the Hudson River. Around the conservatory, garden designer Keith Corlett chose conifers (mainly fir trees) and year-round greenery that would stand up to winter storms. Yews are planted in cedar containers painted white to complement the white of the decorative conservatory structure. The upper and lower terraces are purposely left uncluttered, catching the spirit of the apartment itself, which is the setting for the owner's collection of Gustav Stickley furniture. There are wisteria-covered pergolas on each level, and the more informal upper bedroom terrace is planted with ornamental grasses that are practical and very pleasing to the eye.

A rooftop conservatory

now been replaced with arborvitae.

Bartlett has found that plants do better on her rooftop if planted in masses. This year, roses from all over the garden will be gathered together on the third floor, for effect and to keep the problems in one place. She would like to have a pinetum, and the second floor is moving toward an almost all-green garden. At the moment, plantings include pines, junipers, ferns, boxwood hedges, pyracanthus, climbing hydrangeas, lilacs, and little white birch trees that catch the light. She is trying santolinas and artemisia in pots, wrapping them for winter. On an espaliered pear fence, the twigs are tied down instead of being pruned, with interesting results. She is going to try broom on the top terrace. For a narrow, ground-floor viewing garden, designer Cox brought in evergreen bamboo, the first of a collection of various bamboos. And so, the palette of plants continues to change. Bartlett says the garden is incredibly peaceful. Sometimes she just "sits and watches the grass grow."

An artist experiments

Early in the morning, at lunch time, and at sunset, birds arrive to enjoy this extraordinary garden, and so does the owner, artist Jennifer Bartlett. She often takes a twenty-minute walk around the garden that covers two rooftops of her Greenwich Village studio.

Not just idyllic, the garden is, in fact, a testing ground for the artist's ideas. While Bartlett lived in Europe, she and garden designer Madison Cox researched gardens together. When she returned to New York, she bought a building with large rooftops so she could garden. Cox laid out the framework, quite formal in the European style, and it remains the background for what she calls a pastiche of plantings.

Bartlett has learned a great deal about growing things in shallow containers—some beds are only 9 inches deep. It is her laboratory—she tries anything and everything. Some of the original plantings still exist, but the experimenting goes on. For example, heathers and heaths in the third-floor formal beds did not last, so now there are mounds of inkberry in their place that look like French topiary. She plans to try heathers and heaths again, but in another spot. The yews did not do very well in pots and have

Flowering arches

If a roof terrace is quite narrow, the garden can grow upward instead of outward. Ellen and Michael Schwartz asked garden designer Keith Corlett to give them as much garden as possible on the U-shaped terrace that surrounds their penthouse apartment on Riverside Drive. He devised six metal arches spaced at strategic intervals to frame views of the Hudson River and beyond. The arches, made of metal tubing and anchored in the roof structure, support a vertical garden of climbing vines—mandevilla, wisteria, roses, and clematis twine and flower all summer long. More formal Versailles-style planters hold arborvitae, a beech tree, two Japanese maples, and a cherry tree. These, and an infinite variety of flowering annuals, give the garden exuberant color.

An arboretum

Just a few years ago, when this penthouse terrace with its mature rose garden had to be completely revamped to allow for the installation of new pavers, the owners decided to take a fresh tack. *She* wanted a kind of arboretum of trees not usually found on city terraces. *He* wanted a movable garden of containers and pots that he himself could tend. Together, they called in garden designer Adele Mitchell, who laid out the bones of the garden—mahogany boxes for the trees and trelliswork for climbing vines.

All the woodwork is painted Benjamin Moore's Essex Green enriched with a bit of black. To lighten the load, the boxes have a bottom layer of foam peanuts covered with a fabric or wire membrane to allow for root expansion. Evergreens give the garden interest and structure through the winter season—they include limber pine, 'Oculus Dragonis' pine, 'Blue Star' juniper, 'Jean Dilly' Alberta spruce. Weeping cotoneaster, vibernum, stewartia, paperbark maple, birch, arborvitae, and crab apples offer variety. Among the underplantings are ivies, spreading juniper, nepeta, plumbago, and lobelia. Clematis climbs the trellis. The cascading roses have been returned, to add their luxurious color and scent.

A natural setting

A two-hundred-year-old London plane tree shades this second-floor rooftop. Garden designer Keith Corlett, taking advantage of its wonderful canopy, and keeping in mind the informal atmosphere of Greenwich Village, decided to give the space a natural and airy feeling. He used cedar for the decking, fencing, and the large planters that hold the trees and shrubs. Cedar is lightweight, breathes well, and lightens in color with age. Planters are recessed into the deck to provide more floor space for entertaining. Pots are used for annuals so that they can be moved around easily. Plantings include a weeping birch, weeping maple, ornamental grasses, ferns, variegated ivies, climbing roses, clematis, plumbago, and geraniums. A friend of the owners created the dramatic fountain that flows into the catchment. The effect is cool and refreshing on hot summer days.

A year-round garden

Like a garden beside a country house, the terrace garden of a city apartment adds beauty and is an extension of the dwelling. The eye enjoys it, and the mind uses it to expand one's horizon in every way. The owners of this roof garden asked architects Pietro Cicognani and Ann Kalla to design a solarium to bring more

light inside and enhance the view of the garden outside. Fortunate to have a large area with which to work, Timothy DuVal and project designer Deane Ferrante-Payne of Plant Specialists, Inc., specified plant containers that can be brought in from the perimeters to adjust the space as needed.

Large Japanese hollies

give the sitting area under the awning more privacy, and crab apple trees frame the sunsets and views down Park Avenue. The spiral junipers add a formal touch. Pots are loosely placed about, raised with decorative terra-cotta feet for better air circulation. Plantings are changed seasonally. The owners particularly like aza-

leas, with their vivid purple and red flowers. In the winter, the standing evergreens and the ilex with their red berries are embellished with cut boughs of evergreen, dogwood branches, willow branches, and corkscrew euphorbia. All year long the terrace delights the eye and offers the feeling of escape from the city.

With so many tall buildings encircling their apartment house, Gene and Sara Vogel asked garden designer Keith Corlett to create a roof garden that would give them some privacy but still let them enjoy the spectacular architecture around them.

Three walls of lacy trellis enclose the space and give the feeling of a garden room. Plantings were also chosen for their lacy effects— weeping birches, Japanese maples, Boston ivy, mandevilla, and climbing roses. Three kinds of clematis span the seasons.

Although the garden is not large, there is room for entertaining. The Vogels often breakfast in a wisteria-covered gazebo. Because the garden is not visible from the apartment a floor below, there is no need to have a view of green in wintertime, so very few evergreens are used. During the summer, seasonal plants such as day lilies, impatiens, marguerites, and begonias are brought in to add color and lushness. Designed as an escape into nature, it offers the grand illusion of being out of the city while enjoying all the advantages of city living.

Gardens in Parks

New York City is peppered with parks, plazas, and squares. Two of the grandest, Central Park and Prospect Park, both designed by architects Frederick Law Olmsted and Calvert Vaux, have had a tremendous influence in the world of parks and gardens. Olmsted and Vaux went on to design nearly fifty parks across the country. They were masters of the natural—arranging the greenest of landscapes, mixing rolling meadows and lakes, rocky ledges and streams with small forests of trees.

There is now a great interest in designed flower gardens in parks. Old ones are being renewed, and the basic plans for new parks and park restorations assign important space to them.

The Conservatory Garden in Central Park

The only formal garden in Central Park has an interesting history. The area at Fifth Avenue and 105th Street was planned as an arboretum but later was laid out as a nursery. Glass conservatories, built in 1899, supplied plants to city parks until 1934, when an Italianate plan by M. Betty Sprout, with Gilmore D. Clarke as consulting landscape architect, took their place. The perennial beds were redesigned in 1983 by Lynden B. Miller, now Director of the garden.

The first view through the magnificent gates, made in Paris in 1894 for the Vanderbilt mansion on Fifth Avenue at 58th Street, is a half-acre of manicured lawn flanked by allées of crab apple trees (seen opposite in spring and winter). A wisteria arbor and hedges of yew and spiraea act as a backdrop. The North Garden is a classical design in the French style, with planting beds encircling the Untermyer Fountain of *Three Dancing Maidens* by Walter Schott. In spring, the garden is ablaze with 20,000 tulips given by Mrs. Alexander O. Vietor, and in autumn, with 2,000 chrysanthemum plants

Preceding pages: Spring bulbs in the Conservatory Garden's South Garden

given by the Salute to the Seasons fund, established by Mrs. Albert D. Lasker. During the flowering seasons there is always a great play of color from Japanese quince, the perennial herb lavender cotton, blue pansies, and four rose arbors covered with the white climbing rose 'Silver Moon.'

The South Garden is often referred to as The Secret Garden because of the statue of Mary and Dickon by Bessie Potter ·Vonnoh. The statue, dedicated to Frances Hodgson Burnett, author of the book, stands in a pool of tropical water lilies surrounded with pink 'Betty Prior' roses and dark green winter barberry. There are beds for bulbs and annuals such as snapdragons and nicotiana. Five large beds, redesigned in 1983 by Lynden B. Miller, display 175 different varieties of perennials.

At the southernmost end of the garden is The Woodland Slope, a shade garden of 100 different kinds of perennials and ferns native to America, Europe, and Asia. A restoration of the slope began in 1984, using the planting design of Penelope Maynard. Now, 10,000 plants cover the bank in great drifts of color and contrasting foliage. Those seen here include a pink crab apple tree, daffodils, Virginia bluebells, snowflakes, trilliums, may apples, hellebores, stephanandras, and euonymus.

The Shakespeare Garden in Central Park

The Swedish Cottage, nestled into a hilly part of Central Park where the 79th Street Transverse meets the West Drive, marks an entrance to the Shakespeare Garden. This rustic setting, with its winding paths, leads to romantic Belvedere Castle. Between these two points there is an exuberance of green textures.

In 1987–89, when landscape architects Bruce Kelly and David Varnell worked on the restoration of the garden, the plant lore in Shakespeare's writings was the reference for their plant palette—some 120 varieties were included. Among them are Adonis flower, broom, cuckoo-buds, daffodils, fennel, grape vine, heath, honeysuckle, ivy, lavender, mallow, mulberry, mint, oxslip, primrose, and violets. Together, the plantings are intriguing and the feeling quite magical.

The
Bryant
Park
Gardens

In congested midtown Manhattan, behind the New York Public Library and just a block from Times Square, stands Bryant Park, one of the great rescue stories in the city's history.

It is said the property was earmarked as public space in 1686 by the colonial government. It saw George Washington's army retreat from the British, and was a training ground for Union troops during the Civil War. The Crystal Palace Exhibition was held there in 1853. In 1884 the Park was named for poet-journalist William Cullen Bryant. Thomas Hastings of Carrère & Hastings, architects for the beaux-arts library building, is credited with the architectural design of the garden in 1911. In 1934 it was redesigned by architect Lusby Simpson in a more formal French style.

By the 1980s, the Park, long neglected, had become a hangout for drug dealers and vagrants, a dangerous place after dark. Then the Bryant Park Restoration Corporation was organized to see to the rehabilitation and running of the Park. With money from the city and the private sector, including surrounding buildings, the whole area has been revitalized.

The Park retains much of its original French classical design, with two great allées of plane trees, but important changes make it accessible and inviting. Old entrances have been widened and new ones added. There is more seating, and food is available from kiosks and in a new restaurant. Laurie Olin of Hanna/Olin, Ltd. was the landscape architect for the project and Hugh Hardy of Hardy Holzman Pfeiffer & Associates was the architect for the two gatehouses, food kiosks, and restaurant. Howard Brandston of H. M. Brandston & Partners designed the lighting, including Victorian-style lampposts that outline the edges of the Park at night.

The exuberance and naturalness of two herbaceous gardens, each 300 feet long, contrast with the more formal park structure. A sun garden is to the north side of the great lawn, and to the south there is a shade garden shadowed by plane trees. They were planned by public garden designer Lynden B. Miller. A series of yews and shrubs such as oak-leafed hydrangea, cherry laurels, and spiraea anchor the beds. Spring plantings include tulips, daffodils, and grape hyacinth, hellebores, and digitalis. In midsummer there are numerous varieties of ferns and lilies, coreopsis, hostas, lobelia, and phlox.

Some of the annuals included are ageratum, coleus, heliotrope, hollyhock, nicotiana, salvia, and verbena. In autumn there are ornamental grasses, lobelia, nepeta, rudbeckia, and sedum. The plant list for the gardens is long and always changing. This makes for garden theater. One always looks forward to the gardener's next move.

Gardens in Battery Park City

New land added to the historic New York City waterfront since 1968 is the site of a vital new neighborhood—Battery Park City—at the southernmost tip of Manhattan. Named for the battery of cannons that stood on the shoreline from about 1683 to 1807, it is a residential-business community built on land-fill, much of which came from the excavation for The World Trade Center buildings. Adjoining the financial district, it includes some thirty acres of gardens, parks, plazas, and public spaces, with 1.5 miles of esplanade along the Hudson River.

Landscape architects took part in the early design process, so nature works its magic in this riverbank setting. Leafy trees and flowering shrubs line the promenades, and there are a number of planned gardens. The design of Robert F. Wagner, Jr. Park combines terraced lawns, gardens, and viewing pavilions. The team of landscape architect Laurie Olin, public garden designer Lynden B. Miller, and architects Rodolfo Machado and Jorge Silvetti have created a link between skyscraper and harbor, with uninterrupted views of the Statue of Liberty.

There are two flower gardens in Wagner Park—the North Garden (opposite, above) with warm reds, yellows, and oranges, and the South Garden (right) with cool blues, purples, and pinks. Perennials, annuals, and bulbs, planted in the most luxurious profusion, are chosen in these palettes. For instance, lavender, phlox, daylilies, and asters may be planted with shrub roses, hydrangeas, and butterfly bushes. Both gardens include yew, holly, Japanese maple, and Korean dogwood trees. Evergreens, shrubs, ornamental grasses, barks, and berries give the gardens texture and pattern year round. The South Garden of the World Financial Center (opposite, below) is a contrast of Korean boxwood parterre filled with white birch trees, hostas, and bright red impatiens. It was designed by the landscape architectural firm of M. Paul Friedberg & Partners.

Along the Avenues

The tulips are blooming on Park Avenue, and the cherry trees are flowering at the United Nations—it must be spring. Gardens and art are emerging on city streets, in pocket parks, and on building plazas. Fountains and lights add music and sparkle to city life. Look right, look left, look up. There are gardens where one least expects them. In New York, nature beckons at every turn.

Year round, the malls on Park Avenue are green, and blossoming with lights or flowering color. Each block is a garden. Beds of grass, yew hedges, and a variety of trees keep the malls green. There are flowering cherry, crab apple, and hawthorn trees, and during the winter holiday season fir trees glisten with hundreds of tiny lights. In the spring, beds and planters are brilliant with tulips, and in summer, with begonias, pansies, and impatiens. The Park Avenue Planting Project, Inc., begun in 1980 by Mary Lasker and her Salute to the Seasons Fund, plants and maintains the mall. Buildings on Park Avenue sponsor the Planting Project.

During the summer of 1997, an exhibition of sculpture, "Keith Haring on Park Avenue," was organized by The Public Art Fund and the Whitney Museum of American Art. Shown in the photograph: *Untitled,* 1985, five figures in various colors. Painted aluminum. Collection Eliot K. Wolk. The red-orange dancing figure is *Red Dog,* 1985. Painted steel. Collection Martin and Janet Blinder.

The Park Avenue Malls

Preceding pages: Spring on Park Avenue

Every spring, New Yorkers wait for the cherry trees to bloom in the UN garden on First Avenue at 47th Street. Clouds of pink cherry blossoms cover this famous walk bordered with yellow and white daffodils and ivy. During the 1950s, Mary Lasker, a crusader against cancer and an art collector who loved flowers, arranged for 300 Kwanzan cherry trees and 50,000 daffodils to be planted at the UN in memory of her husband, Albert D. Lasker. In 1957, she formed the Salute to the Seasons Fund for a More Beautiful New York as a way for New Yorkers to contribute to the beautification of the city. Through the years, the Fund has been responsible for hundreds of plantings along avenues and drives, in plazas and parks, and at hospitals and universities throughout the city.

Cherry Walk in

The United Nations Garden

Trees at Trump Tower

Night and day, the eye is drawn to the miniforest on the side of the glass tower at Fifth Avenue and 56th Street. Landscape architect Thomas Balsley, who designed the other garden spaces in the Trump Tower, planted the dramatic architectural setbacks for maximum effect. 'Bradford' pear trees are set in beds of 'Baltica' English ivy that cascades over the edges of the planters. At night the trees gleam with tiny Tivoli lights reflected in the glass facade.

Wisteria on Carnegie Hill

The Romanesque Revival–style facade of the Carnegie Hill townhouse at 17 East 94th Street is at its most decorative when the purple wisteria is in flower. Neighbors of the Ramakrishna-Vivekananda Center of New York wait for the annual blooming, and say young wisterias are sprouting up in their yards, thanks to this robust specimen.

Paley Park

Just a step off Fifth Avenue, at 3 East 53rd Street, there is a much-loved retreat. Opened in 1967, this vest-pocket park was a gift to busy New Yorkers from CBS Chairman William S. Paley in memory of his father.

The plot, about 50 by 100 feet, is like a leafy glade, with shade from honey locust trees and ivy-clad walls. The sound of falling water from the 20-foot-high waterfall softens the city's clamor. There are tables and chairs to move about, and a gatehouse for light refreshments. Large saucers display colorful plants that change with the seasons. The trees seem to spring out of the granite paving stones—a design feature made possible by an underground watering system. Zion & Breen Associates were the site planners and landscape architects for this midtown oasis. A. Preston Moore was the architectural consultant.

Greenacre Park

Not quite an acre, but very green, this small, privately owned park at 221 East 51st Street (between Second and Third Avenues) is open to the public from March through December. Abby Rockefeller Mauzé, who established the Greenacre Foundation, wanted the neighborhood to have a pocket of serenity filled with nature.

Two of the Park's walls are water sculptures. The south wall is a 25-foot-high waterfall that cascades over granite ledges. On the east wall, water gently trickles down the granite to a water channel below. The garden structure, of russet brick and weathered steel, is colorful with rhododendron, azalea, Japanese holly, andromeda, magnolia, and seasonal flowers. The ground cover is pachysandra. Boston ivy on the walls turns a brilliant red in autumn. The park was designed by Hideo Sasaki, former chairman of Harvard's Department of Landscape Architecture, with architect Harmon Goldstone serving as consultant.

Federal Plaza

The idea of a Baroque parterre of Day-Glo green benches and six-foot-high grass mounds swirling across a much-traveled plaza in downtown Manhattan is astonishing. The fact that the plaza is on a garage roof that could not support the weight of trees is not so surprising, but does have a bearing on the daring landscape design. Martha Schwartz, artist, landscape architect, and a professor at Harvard's Graduate School of Design, is known for her imaginative arrangement of public spaces. When she was asked to make the plaza more friendly, pro-viding easy access to the surrounding buildings and plenty of seating for the lunch crowd were high on her list of priorities. Using park elements—benches, lampposts, wire trash baskets, and green grass—Schwartz created a new garden graphic, to the amazement and amusement of New Yorkers accustomed to the picturesque style of Olmsted and Vaux in Central Park. The grass mounds are constructed of lightweight materials and have their own misting system for hot days. Federal Plaza is at the corner of Worth and Lafayette Streets.

Gardens of light

Glowing Topiary Garden

During the 1997–98 holiday season, in New York's financial district, there was a spectacular environmental art installation of light, form, and sound, titled *Glowing Topiary Garden*. This new interpretation of a French topiary garden and a Japanese Zen garden was created by landscape architect Ken Smith and lighting designer Jim Conti in Liberty Plaza Park and was sponsored by the Alliance for Downtown New York. Sixteen translucent cones, sixteen feet tall, and one center cone, twenty-five feet tall, glowed with rainbow colors. Air music was created by 250 wind chimes.

The Park is at Broadway and Liberty Street. During the year, a grove of honey locust trees and beds of coleus and ivy provide shade and color.

Park Avenue Memorial Trees

During the winter holiday season, fir trees encrusted with tiny lights are placed at each end of each block of the Park Avenue malls. They stand on the flower beds, covered with fir boughs, that hold the next spring's tulips. On the first Sunday in December the trees are lighted as a memorial to New Yorkers who have given their lives for their country's freedom in all wars, to celebrate all faiths, and further the cause of peace. The tradition was started in 1945 by Mrs. Stephen C. Clark in memory of her son and other young people who died in World War II. In 1982 the Park Avenue Malls Planting Project, sponsored by the buildings on Park Avenue and Mary Lasker continued the lightings, and in 1983 *Avenue* magazine's Avenue Association joined in. More than two miles of glittering trees is a dazzling sight on a winter's night.

1251 Avenue of the Americas

A spacious entry plaza extends the full block at Sixth Avenue between 49th and 50th Streets in the Rockefeller Center complex. Designed by the architectural firm of Harri-

son & Abramovitz & Harris, the building opened in 1971 and is now owned by Mitsui Fudosan (New York) Inc.

There is a dramatic two-tiered pool with fountains and cascading water. Raised beds are planted with trees and green ground covers. At night, the lighted fountains play amid trees sculptured with tiny lights. The sparkling display carries the dazzle of Radio City Music Hall along the avenue.

Museum Gardens

Art glorifies nature, or is it the other way around? More and more, museums are bringing nature into their galleries and public spaces. Gardens are created to display sculpture, to use in exhibitions, and for special events such as concerts and member receptions.

Nature in a museum setting can work wonders for an indoor space, and the controlled climate of a museum can often be a plus. In an outdoor sculpture garden the elements must be reckoned with. Landscape architects are constantly finding new ways to meet the special challenges of the city.

The Metropolitan Museum of Art

When gardening under glass, without rainstorms and windstorms to stir things up and wash things down, it is necessary to re-create what Mother Nature does outdoors. Fortunately, in the controlled environment of The Metropolitan Museum of Art, the air circulation and humidity regulated for the preservation of works of art also help to maintain the garden plantings.

The courtyard gardens are display gardens. There is always a full fanfare of color and a richness of green year round. Ben Fieman, landscape specialist for the museum, has designed a modular system of lightweight fiberglass containers that are custom-made in a variety of sizes and shapes. These containers fit into wood, metal, or stone planters making up the master design of the gardens. A second set of containers is in the wings ready to be planted with materials at their most glorious display point. Plants are picked and watered by hand. The human touch and constant assessment of needs keeps the gardens fresh and appealing. Like the art, the nature in this museum setting lifts the spirit.

Preceding pages: The Iris and B. Gerald Cantor Roof Garden at the Metropolitan Museum of Art

The Charles Engelhard Court of the American Wing, above, owes its intense green feeling to the pothos ground cover and the ficus trees.

The Carroll and Milton Petrie European Sculpture Court, at left, is lined with ficus trees in classic garden boxes. The center planters, bordered with boxwood hedges, are always filled with blooming plants such as begonias, spathiphyllum, and peace lilies. The sculpture by Francesco Ladatte is Children Playing with Birds of 1745–50.

The Astor Court is a much-admired re-creation of a Ming Dynasty courtyard in a scholar's garden in Suzhou, China. This near-replica of the Late Spring Studio garden court, from the well-known Garden of the Master of the Fishing Nets, was constructed in The Metropolitan Museum of Art by craftsmen from Suzhou, using materials from China and ancient tools and techniques.

The ideas of a Chinese garden have always inspired architects and gardeners—creating a peaceful outdoor place for study and reflection, bringing the essence of the universe into one small space to observe and relish. The principle of the feminine yin and the masculine yang—dark and light, soft and hard—combining in harmonious ways is always present in a Chinese garden. Trees, plants, rocks, water, and architecture are brought together in pleasing arrangements to remind us of the majesty and harmony of nature. There is usually a covered pavilion or walkway for shade, and a place to watch the setting sun and the rising moon.

In the Astor Court, tall, dark river rocks, symbolizing great mountain peaks, are placed against the white walls of the enclosure. Water, a sign of the pure and nourishing, ripples beside the Cold Spring Pavilion with its dramatic upturned roof. Trees, shrubs, and flowering plants, suitable for indoor display, are interpretations of ones found in Chinese paintings. Photographed here are banana trees, black olive, ficus ali, begonia, button and holly fern, liriope. The Astor Court has the timeless qualities of a Chinese garden—beauty, tranquility, nobility.

The Iris and B. Gerald Cantor Roof Garden is bordered with a hedge of yew. This startling all-green frame draws the intense green of Central Park to the viewer's eye. Starting in May there are vines in continual flower—purple wisteria, flame honeysuckle, clematis in jewel colors. White alyssum adds more fragrance, and variegated St. Augustine grass with its white markings adds drama. The bronze figure is *Standing Woman* by Gaston Lachaise, 1927.

The Cloisters

1943, reprinted 1997), had a key role in developing the gardens. Today, Susan Moody, the horticulturist, and her associate Deirdre Larkin see to the design and maintenance, continuing to study gardens and plants of the Middle Ages. They now have a list of more than 300 plants identified through works of art and literature, including a list of herbs from Charlemagne's gardens dated A.D. 812.

The Trie Cloister garden (above) displays plants native to European woodlands and meadows during the Middle Ages, including flora from the Unicorn Tapestries. Daffodils, irises, honesty, wallflowers, Johnny-jump-ups, columbine, and daisies are some of the flowers one is apt to see. Trees include holly and pomegranate. The center fountain, a composite of two late fifteenth- to early sixteenth-

One of the world's greatest collections of medieval art and horticulture can be seen at The Cloisters in Fort Tryon Park, high above the Hudson River. This extraordinary assemblage of art and architecture, including five Romanesque and Gothic cloisters from France, is a branch of The Metropolitan Museum of Art.

A gift from John D. Rockefeller, Jr., enabled the museum to buy a collection of medieval architectural artifacts from the American sculptor George Grey Barnard. Rockefeller also gave the land, financed the construction, and contributed medieval art from his own collection, including the glorious Unicorn Tapestries. To protect the view, he bought the land across the river and gave it to New York State. Architect Charles Collens and curator James J. Rorimer saw the pro-

ject to completion in 1938.

The museum is home to both religious and secular art dating from the twelfth through the fifteenth centuries—sculpture, illuminated manuscripts, the work of goldsmiths and silversmiths, and the Unicorn Tapestries—many of which

have inspired plantings in the Cloister gardens. Margaret B. Freeman, a curator and author of the books *The Unicorn Tapestries* (Metropolitan Museum of Art, 1943, reprinted 1976) and *Herbs for the Medieval Household* (Metropolitan Museum of Art,

century limestone elements, is a bird's delight.

The Bonnefont Cloister, (opposite, below) looking south along the Hudson River, is the main teaching garden. Everything is labeled and there are guided tours of the plantings. Under the quince trees are woodland plants such as fern, columbine, and ragged robin. Raised beds surrounded by brick pathways are devoted to plants grown for a particular use. The aromatic bed is fragrant with lavender, lemon balm, and meadowsweet. The bed of artist's materials includes madder, weld, and ward—which produced the red, yellow, and blue dyes, respectively, for the Unicorn Tapestries. Salad greens such as tansy, lovage, field pea, and sorrel fill the kitchen bed. In the medicinal bed there is comfrey, germander (a type of mint), and foxglove. The decorative wellhead and the wattle fences are typical of those in a medieval monastery garden. Just outside the south wall there is a crab apple orchard.

The Cuxa Cloister (above) surrounds a garth—a small enclosed courtyard open to the sky and laid out in a formal manner with crossed paths and a center fountain. Crab apple, cornelian cherry, pear, and hawthorn trees are set in grassy squares and edged with flowering borders that include spiraea, astilbe, Russian sage, salvia, balloonflower, bleeding heart, anemone, and various bulb flowers. In the autumn, the garden is brilliant with the blue-purple of New York asters. Tubs of citrus trees, bay, and jasmine are moved out and in with the seasons. The cloister garden is patterned after a medieval monastic garden, where monks strolled and contemplated the wonders of nature.

The Museum of Modern Art

In 1953, architect Philip Johnson restructured a small garden at The Museum of Modern Art, and it was named The Abby Aldrich Rockefeller Sculpture Garden in memory of one of the Museum's founders. In 1964, Johnson was the architect for a major expansion. Landscape architect James Fanning was a consultant for the first garden, and Zion & Breen Associates for the second.

There is a sense of order and serenity to the garden, yet it is never boring. The visual impact constantly changes with the light and the seasons. It is a pleasure to walk among the plantings and over the two water channels, viewing the sculptures from all sides. The stepping stones are Vermont

marble squares which in themselves set a pattern. Trees cast dappled shadows that move with the breeze—weeping beech, cut-leaf birch, little-leaf linden, and London plane trees. The beds are English ivy. Color is brought in seasonally with tulips, pansies, coreopsis, or chrysanthemums.

It is a most splendid outdoor sculpture gallery. The view from above, looking northeast, shows Miro's *Moonbird* (1966) and Calder's *Black Widow* (1959). In the view opposite is Elie Nadelman's *Man in the Open Air*, (c. 1915).

The garden, visible from all floors of the museum, is often the setting for receptions and concerts. On a summer's night, it is one of the treasures of the city.

Cooper-Hewitt, National Design Museum

Museum of the Smithsonian Institution.

In 1992, when the garden was to be renovated, garden designers Mary Riley Smith and Lynden B. Miller were brought in. Retaining the original garden and path layout, they designed new plantings. With the help of a number of volunteers from the Central Park Conservatory Garden, this luxurious stretch of Fifth Avenue began to bloom again. Mary Riley Smith and five or six volunteers, who contribute their time every week from April through November, plus two part-time paid gardeners continue the work. Now, visitors to outdoor exhibitions and special events in the Arthur Ross Terrace and Garden enjoy three lush new flower areas. Four thousand tulip bulbs start the season, followed by annuals and perennials—phlox, salvias, verbenas, perillas. There are large Norway maples and chestnuts around the perimeter, with barberry shrubs and other plantings such as hostas, ferns, and hydrangeas. The wonder of the garden is a purple wisteria, rampant over the south face of the building. It is believed to date from the very first garden planted as the century began. Even for the passersby, the garden is a great refreshment.

At the turn of this century there were a number of gardens attached to family mansions along Fifth Avenue. The spacious garden of the Carnegie Mansion is a reminder of how rural the Upper East Side of New York City was when steel baron Andrew Carnegie bought the property in 1898. Architects Babb, Cook, and Willard designed a comfortable sixty-four-room house for the Carnegies, and Schermerhorn & Foulks laid out the garden that runs the full block from 90th to 91st Street. After Louise Carnegie's death in 1946, the house was used by Columbia University. In 1968 the property became the Cooper-Hewitt Museum, now the National Design

On Staten Island's Lighthouse Avenue, there is a museum devoted to the culture and arts of Tibet. Founded in 1945 by Asian art dealer Edna Klauber, whose professional name was Jacques Marchais, it houses her collection and furthers the study and understanding of Tibetan and other Asian civilizations.

Designed in the spirit of a small Tibetan mountain temple, the museum has a terraced garden with a view of Lower New York Bay. Plants native to the Himalayas are featured—rhododendrons, azaleas, peonies, irises, and roses—as well as a prized Tibetan orange tree. Shaded by mature evergreens and paved with colorful flagstones, it is the setting for three Buddhas, including the white marble Burmese one shown here. Ground covers are mostly pachysandra and myrtle. A small replica of an Asian elephant displays an upturned trunk, symbol of good luck. There is a goldfish pond with water lilies and lotus. The lotus appears often in Asian art, and flowers embellish the tankas, Tibetan scroll paintings used in meditation at Tibetan altars. The beauty of the art and the naturalness of the plantings create a serene garden.

The Jacques Marchais Museum of Tibetan Art

The Isamu Noguchi Garden Museum

Sculptor Isamu Noguchi once wrote: "When the time came for me to work with larger spaces, I conceived them as gardens, not as sites with objects but as relationships to a whole. I would say this came from my knowledge of the dance theater, where there is evidently a totality of experience by the audience.

"Through gardens I came to a deeper awareness of nature and of stone. The natural boulders of hard stone—basalt, granite, and the like—which I now use are a congealment of time. They are old. But are they old as sculpture?"

Noguchi's garden museum, in the borough of Queens, is an amazing place in which to view a comprehensive collection of his work. It was created by the artist and dedicated in 1985, three years before his death. An outgrowth of his studio, which he moved to Long Island City in the early sixties to be near the marble suppliers on Vernon Boulevard, the museum houses works he retained for himself through the years. His passionate involvement with nature, his heritage, and the influences of his life in New York and Japan come together here.

The garden reflects his great interest in stage design and his experience of designing sets for the Martha Graham dance company for many years. The brilliance of sculpting space with rocks, stone, water, trees, and shrubs, enhancing the spirit of his own work, is evident.

Some elements of the traditional Japanese garden are interpreted in this setting of white birch, weeping cherry, katsura, magnolia, black pine, and ailanthus trees, bamboo, juniper, Boston and English ivies.

In his book, *The Isamu Noguchi Garden Museum*, Noguchi wrote: "For me it is the direct contact of artist to material which is original, and it is the earth and his contact to it which will free him from the artificiality of the present." (Harry N. Abrams, Inc., Publishers, New York, 1987.)

The Frick Collection

The French-style eighteenth-century mansion that houses Henry Clay Frick's magnificent collection of European art was completed in 1914. It became one of New York's most enjoyable museums in 1935. The east reception room and the garden enclosure, influenced by Le Grand Trianon at the Palace of Versailles, were added in 1977.

Russell Page, the English landscape gardener responsible for the restoration of a number of formal gardens in France, was called in to lay out the garden. As the man on site, he hired garden designer Galen Lee, who continues as the Frick's Horticulturist. Lee tells us that Page planned the space as a viewing garden.

He raised the garden 3 feet above street level, which gives the passerby a fascinating perspective, very different from that of the reception room. The limestone walls with their decorative elements called for a formal plan, and the pool is the focus, with green lawn and ornamental gravel paths continuing the symmetry. English boxwood borders the beds, with mounds of Korean boxwood flanking the water lily pool that also includes tall lotus. White wisteria and many varieties of clematis thrive on the trellis arches. In the north beds there are azaleas and rhododendron in pink and white. Dwarf hollies, astilbe, blue scilla, and columns of blue plumbago fill the east beds. Trees include redwood, crab apple, and flowering cherry. The south beds are filled with white tulips, but the colors in the beds change yearly, and sometimes include the soft reds and lavenders of an Impressionist's palette. The background remains the same, but the scene is always changing.

Japan Society

In 1907, the Japan Society was founded in New York to further understanding between the United States and Japan. Today, the Society continues its work with art exhibitions, programs for the performing arts, educational workshops, and symposiums on issues of interest to both countries. The Society's home is in a handsome building on East 47th Street, designed by Tokyo architect Junzo Yoshimura, which opened in 1971. Two new indoor gardens were created on the second floor of a three-story atrium during a 1997 renovation. With soothing sound and gentle movement, water flows along a slate channel and then to a pool garden on the floor below. Zion & Breen Associates, the landscape architects, chose elements from a traditional Japanese garden to use in their contemporary design: bamboo, water, and stone. The yellow bamboo is 'Aura.' The Boston fern ground cover is 'Compacta.'

Urasenke Tea Ceremony Society

In an old carriage house on the Upper East Side of Manhattan, the Urasenke Tea Ceremony Society maintains a serene Japanese garden. Designed by Kyoto architect Teruhiko Negishi in 1980, it links rooms where the art of the tea ceremony is taught and practiced.

The garden contains many traditional elements—stepping-stones, rocks, a bamboo gate, a stone basin, and a stone lantern. A teahouse garden is planted only with green, never color. Here, where there is no direct sunlight, the plantings include mosses, ferns, creeping fig, and aglaonema.

Historic House Gardens

Period gardens, like period rooms, have a story to tell. New York City is fortunate to have a number of museum houses with gardens that reflect their time and architectural style. The designs and plantings give visitors great pleasure and good ideas to take home to their own gardens.

Bartow-Pell Mansion Museum

Preceding pages and above: The water garden at the Bartow-Pell Mansion Museum

Thomas Pell, an English doctor, bought a 50,000-acre tract from the Siwanoy Indians in 1654. He built a manor house on Long Island Sound, in what is now Pelham Bay Park in the Bronx, and four generations of Pells lived there until the American Revolution, when the house was burned. A Pell descendant, Robert Bartow, bought the property in 1836 and built the present mansion, which remained in family hands until 1888, when it was acquired by the city. In 1914, the International Garden Club, Inc., leased the house and garden for its headquarters and for horticultural purposes.

Architect William Delano, of Delano & Aldrich, became involved in the restoration of the Federal-style house and designed the terraced garden. Enclosed by walls and iron fences, the garden is divided in quadrants by stone paths and steps. At the center is a water garden with lilies, lotus, lettuce plants, floating hyacinth, and goldfish. Six handsome yew trees are placed symmetrically around the pool, and surrounding beds are bright with zinnias and dahlias. Geraniums and ivy fill giant stone urns, and there are roses at the gates.

The Gracie Mansion Conservancy

The official residence of the Mayor of the City of New York takes its name from Scottish ship owner Archibald Gracie, who bought the property in 1798 and built the Federal-style country house the following year. Situated in Carl Schurz Park, at 88th Street and East End Avenue, the house has a large flower garden and a woodland garden. In 1984, landscape architect Phillip Winslow designed the grounds and gardens to reflect original plantings shown in early prints. Chestnut, apple, and willow trees were added. Brick paths and planting areas were designed.

The front flower beds are planted with perennials, annuals, tender bulbs, and hardy bulbs that bloom from spring to autumn. Among the flowers shown here: Madonna lilies, summer hyacinth, catnip, and verbena. There is also a woodland garden entered through gates set in a wall of yew. Some of the shade-loving plants there are hostas, myrtle, oakleaf hydrangeas, and Siberian bugloss.

Dyckman Farmhouse Museum

Jan Dyckman immigrated from Westphalia around 1662 and began to acquire land in what is now upper Manhattan. At its peak, the farm was 450 acres, one of the largest estates in the city's history. It remained in the family until 1871. During the Revolution, British and Hessian troops were encamped there. After the Dyckmans returned in 1784, they built the present house in the Dutch Colonial style at what is now 4881 Broadway. It is the last of its kind in Manhattan. Two sisters, direct descendants of Jan Dyckman, purchased the house in 1915, restored it, and gave it to the city.

The garden was designed by Alexander MacMillan Welch in 1916, when the Museum was created. It has the spirit of a traditional Dutch patterned garden, with symmetrical flower beds edged in boxwood. In the center, there is a magnolia tree. Flowering plants in the outer borders include peonies, roses, hostas, iris, hollyhocks, and daylilies.

The Abigail Adams Smith Museum

This museum house, at 421 East 61st Street, reflects its life as a hotel in the early 1800s. However, it was built in 1799 as a carriage house by Colonel William Stephens Smith and his wife Abigail, daughter of President John Adams. The house went through various hands until 1924, when it was purchased by the Colonial Dames of America, who manage and maintain its collections of American decorative arts.

The garden, laid out in an eighteenth-century style by landscape architect Alice R. Ireys in 1972, is enclosed in a Colonial board fence decorated with diamonds of English ivy. Along the fence are pleached oriental plane trees with circular beds of ivy, and in the spring, cottage tulips. There is a patterned flower garden and an herb garden. Some of the early plant materials used in the garden are shadblush, laurel, mock orange, viburnum, and flowering quince. The spring underplantings include snowdrops, violets, primulas, and coral bells. Recently, landscape architect Gina Ingoglia Weiner, garden adviser to the Museum, added a stepping-stone path and a small native woodland garden.

In 1832, Joseph Brewster built a handsome house in late Federal style for his family at 29 East 4th Street. It was their home for three years, until Seabury Tredwell, a successful hardware merchant, bought it. The Tredwells lived there until 1933. In 1936, the house was opened to the public as a house museum. Its Greek Revival interior and original furnishings reflect the life of a nineteenth-century merchant family in the city.

What is now the garden was once a grassy yard used for deliveries and drying laundry. Today, an assortment of vines decorate its walls: wisteria, Virginia creeper, Boston ivy, Concord grape, and climbing sweet pea. Head Gardener John W. Rummel sees that the flower beds are a mix like an English border, including bleeding hearts, hostas, lilies, heliotrope, alyssum, boxwood, and junipers. The iron furniture adds a Victorian touch.

Morris-Jumel Mansion

The imposing residence atop a height at 65 Jumel Terrace was built in 1765 as a summer villa for British Colonel Roger Morris and his American wife, Mary Philipse. He was the son of Roger Morris, a noted English architect who worked in the Palladian style. The Morris family fled during the Revolution, and General Washington used the house for a time as his headquarters. French émigré merchant Stephen Jumel and his wife, Eliza, bought the mansion in 1810 and furnished it in French Empire style, and in the Mansion's collections are some Napoleonic pieces of furniture.

The house was opened as a museum in 1907, but it was not until 1935 that the present garden and garden house were installed by the WPA. The octagonal sunken garden, more herbs than flowers, is surrounded with sycamores and American elms dating from the 1800s, and with wild rose bushes. A boxwood hedge encircles a formal rose garden.

The Stephens-Prier House at Historic Richmond Town

Daniel Lake Stephens, a native Staten Islander, built this Italianate frame house in 1858. In 1992, it was acquired by the Richmond Town Restoration, a historic village in La Tourette Park that encompasses 100 acres and has 28 historic buildings spanning three centuries.

The current gardens of the Stephens-Prier House were begun in 1992 by Barnett Shepherd, Executive Director of the Staten Island Historical Society. The design and plantings were selected to complement the house's nineteenth-century architecture. The oval perennial garden includes daylilies, lamb's ears, statice, lantana, salvia, and hollyhocks. A vegetable garden has geometric beds, brick paths, and small boxwoods at the center.

Gardens at the Office

Gardens are a growing part of the business landscape. Architects and designers are finding new ways to use nature, for the beauty of a garden enriches and nourishes. It appears that putting nature to work is good business.

Seven stories aboveground, on the rooftops of the Rockefeller Center buildings, along Fifth Avenue, there are four spectacular gardens that can be seen from over 100,000 windows in surrounding buildings. The gardens were planned as an integral element when the Center was built, so the roofs were well insulated and covered with two feet of planting soil. British landscape designer Ralph Hancock planned and installed the gardens in the early 1930s. The effect is of classical parterres—lawns of rolled Kentucky bluegrass, clipped yew hedges, evergreens pruned in cone shapes, turquoise reflecting pools, stone planters and terracotta pots filled with pink geraniums. A good place from which to see the gardens is the café on the seventh floor of Saks Fifth Avenue.

The famous street-level Channel Gardens, between La Maison Française and the British Empire Building, are designed along reflecting pools with rollicking triton and nereid fountains. Shown here is an installation that includes palm trees, bromeliads, and coryline. New Yorkers look forward to the change of plantings that takes place every two or three weeks under the watchful eye of Rockefeller Center Horticulturist Dave Murbach. The year ends in a blaze of lighted angels that lead to the spectacular Rockefeller Center holiday tree.

Preceding pages: Roof garden at Rockefeller Center

Gardens for the view

An alpine
trough garden

What is said to be the largest trough garden in the world sits on a rooftop in Rockefeller Center. Eighty-three troughs are arranged on two terraces, each approximately 200 feet long. They are botanical gardens in miniature and contain more than 600 species and cultivars, including dwarf trees, shrubs, perennials, annuals, bulbs, and grasses. Unusual alpines and rare species from Asia and Africa are highlights.

When the corporate identity firm of Siegel & Gale, Inc., leased the space, they asked Susan Keiser of Greystone Gardens to create a garden they could enjoy from indoors as well as out, one that would grow and change with the seasons and look good year round. Considering weather conditions and rooftop weight restrictions, the idea of an alpine trough garden, popular in the nineteenth century, was reborn. Here, the troughs are made of fiberglass instead of the traditional stone, and are anchored in beds of Timberline, a lightweight mulching material. Five different sizes of troughs are placed on bases at two different levels and arranged in an interesting pattern. Each trough is unique, a composition of dwarf plantings and chunks of Tufa rock, an ideal growing medium for alpines.

Bringing nature to the office

The challenge here was to transform a large, black tar roof into a garden to give the staff of the Hearst Corporation headquarters something green and wonderful to look at all year long. When Gilbert C. Maurer, Executive Vice-President and Chief Operating Officer, realized the potential of the rooftop space of this newer section of the building, he

called in garden designer Mary Riley Smith. The result is a formal viewing garden in the French style. As part of the master plan, a courtyard garden below was restored to its original Art Deco design and is now used for employee lunches and corporate parties.

After engineers determined the roof weight limits, including snow loads, steel beams were added to the three exposed sides for reinforcement. With the assistance of landscape architect Donna Gutkin, a layout was devised to suit the superstructure of the roof. Air-handling machines were enclosed in 6-foot-high trellis fences painted a deep green. Thirty cedar planters were constructed, including a huge one only 5 inches deep, to hold the green lawn.

Plantings are mostly evergreen: yew, holly, boxwood, and English ivy. The pyramids of green are Japanese holly that can be sheared in ornamental shapes. Japanese dogwood, with its interesting bark in winter, is decorative year round. Early summer annuals such as impatiens and cascading geraniums add a dash of color to the greenery.

The dramatic center of the garden is an eagle, the Hearst symbol cast in bronze, that appears to be landing on the splashing fountain. The look of the garden changes with the shifting light throughout the day and throughout the year.

A working terrace

One of the most innovative New York real estate developers in the 1920s, Fred F. French, built a building for himself at 551 Fifth Avenue which housed his company and his private living quarters. The building has an ornate lobby and unusual faience decorations on the facade at the top. When the firm of American Industrial Partners took office space in the building—said to be part of the French apartment— they gained a terrace and a piece of built-in art. Garden designer Mary Riley Smith was asked to arrange the terrace so the partners could sit outside and enjoy the tremendous view. She brought in teak furniture and planters that would stand up to changeable weather. The containers are lushly planted with junipers, roses, and blue spruce. A trellis of clematis and honeysuckle adds color and fragrance.

Calm and collected

A compelling design based on Ryoan-ji, the Zen rock garden in Kyoto, Japan, is the solution Jeff Mendoza found for this seventeenth-floor tar-paper roof. He created the first version of the garden in 1985 for a previous tenant, and when the new occupant, an advertising agency, moved in, he had the opportunity to refine his design. The agency took the space in this down-town building off Fifth Avenue because they liked the gar-den, and encouraged Men-doza's revamping plan.

Now the roof is a serene composition of rectangular patterns. Mendoza was a sculptor before he took up gardening some twenty years ago, so material and form are important in his work. A lightweight metal frame, with planting troughs only four inches deep, supports the garden above the roof. The center recess is filled with Japanese river pebbles, and a border with river rocks. Some plantings are new, and some of the original ones have been rearranged.

The narrow edging of green is sedum, and there is pen-nisetum in the copper boxes. Sculpted wall planters are filled with boxwood. A speci-men weeping pine adds drama.

Thinking of the busy, cre-ative atmosphere of the office inside, Mendoza wanted the eye to rest, not roam, in this viewing garden. By limiting the elements, he achieved the minimalist feeling he envi-sioned.

Bamboo and sculpture

The glass atrium of the former IBM building, designed by architect Edward Larabee Barnes in 1982, is now the Sculpture Garden at 590 Madison Avenue. The landscape firm of Zion & Breen designed the bamboo garden. The building's new owners asked architect Robert A. M. Stern to redesign the atrium to accommodate large works of outdoor sculpture. Four exhibitions a year are presented. Shown here, among the stands of black bamboo, is Bryan Hunt's bronze *Crossing,* of 1995.

A garden under glass

The Winter Garden at the World Financial Center in Battery Park City is a heroic interpretation of the traditional palm court. Rising 120 feet, this vaulted glass hall facing the Hudson River is home to a grove of Washingtonia robusta palm trees. Sixteen of these native American palms, their tall trunks topped with lush, umbrellalike fronds, resemble columns in this dramatic public space. Cesar Pelli was the architect and Diana Balmori was the landscape designer.

Office and garden are one

One of the Ford Foundation's many gifts to New York is the garden court of its headquarters at 320 East 43rd Street, which is open to the public during working hours. The glass-and-steel structure soars 160 feet into the sky with offices on two sides. The greenest of gardens cascades down three levels to a center pool, bringing nature to offices on all floors.

The twelve-story greenhouse was the idea of architects Kevin Roche and John Dinkeloo, who created this garden court on almost a third of an acre. The landscape architect for the project was Dan Kiley. Inspired by the geometry of natural landscapes, Kiley, who speaks of his designs as multidimensional, like a walk in nature, brought these ideas to the Ford space. The plants used are mostly indigenous to the South and the Caribbean, including bougainvillea, ficus, pines, podocarpus, eucalyptus, black olive, and weeping fig. The plantings have been maintained for many years by John Mini Indoor Landscapes. Flowers are changed with the seasons.

Healing gardens

The Joel Schnaper Memorial Garden, at the Terence Cardinal Cooke Health Care Center on upper Fifth Avenue, was designed for residents with AIDS and their families by David Kamp of Dirtworks, Inc. He believes that nature is an agent of healing, and gardens enhance nature's inherent restorative qualities.

The sixth-floor terrace garden is divided into small sitting areas by lattices, trellises, and a tent pavilion. There is a giant sundial painted on the terrace floor. A wisteria vine covers the entrance, and clematis arches over the windows. Plantings include vegetables, herbs, and dwarf fruit trees. Some of the colorful flowers are hibiscus, lantana, dahlias, heliotrope, and jasmine. Residents often add their own plants and tend them. Fragrant plants, foliage that flutters in the breeze, and music from tinkling wind chimes add to the healing atmosphere of the garden.

The Enid A. Haupt Glass Garden at The Howard A. Rusk Institute of Rehabilitation Medicine on East 34th Street is a place for delight, for therapy, and for education. Designed for patients and their families, it is open to the public and is wheelchair accessible. The glass conservatory was custom designed by specialists Lord & Burnham and displays plants that do well in a warm, therapeutic atmosphere—aquatic plants, ferns, palms, bromeliads, orchids, cacti, and succulents. Tropical birds and fish add brilliant color. Other sections include a greenhouse for plants that adapt well to low light and dry city dwellings, an outdoor perennial garden designed by the architectural firm of Kelly/Varnell, Inc., and a children's garden that brings play, therapy, and learning together in a natural setting.

Hidden Enclaves

Sprinkled across the city are private spaces of architectural interest with wonderful gardens. There are courtyards and small parks, tended and enjoyed by the residents around them, that can be seen as one passes by. And, there are campuses and closes rich in history that are open to the public at certain times or that can be toured by special arrangement.

On these pages: On Grove Street, between Bedford and Hudson in the West Village, there are six Federal-style houses arranged on a garden court. Grove Court consists of attached frame-and-brick houses that were built as working-class housing in the 1830s. It is said that O. Henry wrote his short story "The Last Leaf" there in 1907. The lush bed of ivy and the leafy green trees and shrubs are striking against the red-and-white facades.

An apartment garden court

This Italianate building on the Upper East Side was built in 1930 by John D. Rockefeller, Jr., as apartments for scientists and doctors working at Rockefeller University. The facade is decorated with animal and floral carvings, and the arched entrances have handsomely carved columns. A well in the center courtyard originally held water and now spills over with bright pink impatiens. Honeysuckle grows on the well frame, and the hedge around it is euonymus. Some of the original plantings remain, including ilex, laurel, azalea, rhododendron, and English holly. Moss, ferns, pachysandra, and hosta have been added.

Pomander Walk

Tudor-style houses in a play by Louis N. Parker prompted developer Thomas Healy to build Pomander Walk, a mews on West 94th Street, in 1921. The play's title, *Pomander Walk,* was taken from a street in the London suburb of Cheswick. The firm of King & Campbell modeled the twenty-seven houses after the stage set, and Healy offered them to theater professionals. Humphrey Bogart was one of the early occupants. The two-story, brightly trimmed little houses are a delightful surprise amid the tall apartment buildings. Window boxes and doorstep plots are tended by each tenant. The variety and randomness of plantings give the walk the look of a carefree English border garden.

Sniffen Court

Preceding pages: Sniffen Court has always been a favorite of artists and writers. Sculptor Malvina Hoffman had a studio in this East 36th Street mews of brick carriage houses (1850–60), and the first building on the right is home to the Amateur Comedy Club, a private theatrical group founded 113 years ago. The stone courtyard is like a garden, green with vines, small trees, and evergreen shrubs. Window boxes and doorstep planters spill over with impatiens, petunias, and begonias. One can enjoy the garden while passing by the gate.

Gramercy Park

The land now known as Gramercy Park was bought by Peter Stuyvesant in 1651 from the Dutch West India Company. In 1831, Samuel B. Ruggles purchased the acreage from a Stuyvesant descendant and divided it into building lots around a private park, creating the Gramercy Park Trust. A gardener, James Virtue, was hired by the Park trustees in the spring of 1838, and some of his bills for trees and shrubs still survive. On his lists are horse chestnuts,

sugar maples, tulip trees, English lindens, snowballs, Persian lilacs, magnolias, and dogwoods. In 1992, landscape architects Quennell-Rothschild Associates began working on a plan for the park's rehabilitation, which is in progress.

The Park is divided into quadrants, bordered by boxwood and planted with grass, ivy, and bulbs. The perimeter beds are informal woodland or shade gardens with small crab apples, hawthorns, and dogwoods, with a variety of

shrubs including viburnum, rhododendron, azaleas, mountain laurel, and cotoneaster. Around a statue of actor Edwin Booth (dressed as Hamlet) there is a new rose garden that was designed by Stephen Scanniello, noted

rosarian at the Brooklyn Botanic Garden.

Owners of property in the Gramercy Park Trust and residents have keys to the Park, but it can be seen and enjoyed by all who walk by.

The Rockefeller University

This respected center for scientific research and graduate education, founded in 1901, occupies land purchased by John D. Rockefeller, Jr., in 1903. Today, the fifteen-acre campus is much admired for the plantings, formal gardens, and fountains designed in 1956 by landscape architect Dan Kiley. The serenity of the garden is attributable to Kiley's treatment of the landscape as a formal, symmetrical design linking the university buildings. Shown here are walks bordering the Great Lawn, shaded by London plane trees some of which date from 1910, flowering crab apple trees, and mountain laurel. The sculpture is Minoru Nuzuma's marble *Mouth of River,* 1966.

The campus is mainly a landscape of woody ornamentals. In the Dome Garden there are four circular fountains, a large bed of clipped Japanese hollies, and azaleas. Trees include Blue Atlas cedar and Japanese cedar. The Philosopher's Garden, a quiet seating area with two fountains, is just beyond. Niloufar Leibel is the horticultural consultant to the University.

General Theological Seminary

The oldest Episcopal seminary in the United States was founded in 1817 but did not move to its present site at 171 Ninth Avenue, in the Chelsea district of Manhattan, until 1927. Clement Clarke Moore, the Biblical language professor who wrote *The Night Before Christmas,* gave his old apple orchard to the church for the campus.

The close, completed in 1902, still retains much of its pastoral feeling, with broad green lawns and old oak, maple, ginkgo, and London plane trees. Virginia creeper decorates some of the brick buildings, and ground covers include English, American, and Japanese hollies, boxwood, cherry laurels, yew, and lily-of-the-valley shrub. A perennial garden, shown looking toward the bell tower of the Chapel of the Good Shepherd, is planted with many varieties, including ornamental alliums, daylilies, and peonies. Annie Gower is Head of Horticulture for the Seminary. The garden is open to the public for a few hours each day except Sunday. Passersby can see part of the campus on 20th Street.

The Cathedral of St. John the Divine

The largest church in the United States, this remarkable edifice is in the Morningside Heights section of the city, at Amsterdam Avenue and 112th Street. The principal church for the Episcopal Diocese of New York was incorporated in 1873, and ground was broken for the building in 1892.

The church's thirteen-acre close is considered to be Manhattan's largest private park accessible to the public. It includes a Peace Fountain and a Biblical Garden of plants, trees, and shrubs mentioned in the Bible. The Hope Rosary Garden has one of the nation's largest collections of 'David Austin' roses. A garden planted with 7,200 bulbs, including tulips, hyacinths, narcissi, and irises, is a memorial to Kathryn Speicher-Dunham, and foxgloves bloom in the southwest corner of the close

in tribute to the artist Keith Haring. Shown here, the Gothic-style Deanery with its own delightful garden that flowers with yarrow, lavender, foxglove, daylilies, and more, is encircled by hostas, ferns, buddleia, and dogwood. The forty-foot-high Gothic pulpit of Daytona stone, designed by Howell and Stokes, stands like a piece of sculpture in the center of the Bishop's lawn. Maria Hernandez is the horticulturist for the close.

Community Gardens

In all five boroughs of New York City there are hundreds of small garden plots, and some not so small, that are tended by neighborhood groups. Flowers, fruits, and vegetables thrive under the loving care of residents who come together to beautify surroundings that, in most cases, are in definite need of beautifying. In New York, the term "community garden" is generally applied to a garden on city-owned vacant property on loan to the neighborhood. In recent years, some have been designated parks. There are also plots on property not owned by the city where neighbors gather to garden.

Since 1978, New York City's GreenThumb has licensed over a thousand lots to some 750 community groups. A program funded by federal Community Development Block Grants, it is the largest municipally run community gardening program in the United States. GreenThumb also helps neighborhood groups by supplying tools, soil, and lumber, and assists with the design process, seeking to meet each group's particular needs. Education is an important part of the effort. For example, workshops and an annual conference bring gardeners together, and community-built gardens in school yards are used as outdoor classrooms. There are other city programs and privately funded organizations that reach out to community gardeners—the botanical gardens, The Horticultural Society of New York, and the Green Guerillas among them. (A list of these resources is available from Green Thumb, 49 Chambers Street, Room 1020, New York, New York, 10007. Telephone 212-788-8059.)

Community gardens are usually fenced in, with keys issued to gardeners and neighbors involved in their programs. Most can be seen from the sidewalk, and signs post times when they are open to the public. Many have individual raised beds, filled with fresh, uncontaminated soil, that are allotted to families to grow their own crops of vegetables and flowers. Common areas are used for various activities, such as block association meetings, wedding receptions, fund-raising picnics, tours for children or the handicapped, nutrition classes, exhibitions, lectures, and concerts. The gardens are often organized as nonprofit entities, with volunteers and steering committees seeing to the design and maintenance of the gardens and raising money for further development.

The tremendous power of things green and flowering is always amazing. The atmosphere of a whole city can be changed block by block. Joining together to grow food, medicinal herbs, trees, and plants brings rewards of friendship, safety, and many other pleasures.

On these pages: Liz Christy Bowery Houston Garden, 110 East Houston Street. This community garden was started by Liz Christy in 1972. She went on to found other greening organizations, including the Green Guerillas.

The garden of the Golden Lion, 263 West 121st Street between Seventh and Eighth Avenues, was founded by the nearby Ethiopian Orthodox Coptic Church and a tenants association. The sign was painted by the Bishop of the church.

Brisas la Caribe, 237 East 3rd Street, between B and C Avenues, was started by enthusiatic neighbors in 1992 to grow flowers and vegetables. There is an open casita where they can sit and admire their work. Roses and a scarecrow add color to the scene.

9th Street Community Garden and Park, at the northeast corner of 9th Street at Avenue C, was started in 1979. This community garden is one of the largest in the city. In addition to common areas with paths and seating, seventy-two neighborhood volunteers each have a 10-by-10-foot space in which to create their own gardens. The wishing well, created by Xavier Rodriguez of found materials, is covered with 'Blaze' roses. The planted island is a mix of begonias, itea, thistles, artichokes, and more. The serpentine brick path leads through a wisteria-covered trellis to a small secret garden.

Lotus Garden, West 97th Street between Broadway and West End Avenue. A second-story garden created in 1983, this green expanse atop a garage belonging to the Columbia Condominium shows a neighborhood group's success in working with a commercial builder to include a community garden in the plans. Lotuses bloom in the fish pond, and some thirty volunteers tend the flowers, herbs, fruit trees, and vines.

Carlton Garden, on Carlton Avenue between Fulton and Green Streets, Brooklyn. Twenty-five families grow vegetables, herbs, and flowers on what used to be two vacant lots. The wall painting by artist Janet Braun-Reinetz includes a mantis, a symbol of good luck.

Opposite: The 6 B–C Botanical Garden, 634 East 6th Street between Avenues B and C, is divided into flower garden, rock garden, cactus garden, shade garden, and herb garden. An area for meditation includes a Chinese teahouse and lantern.

Holy Rosary, 119 Pleasant Street, was sponsored by the Holy Rosary Church and started in 1992. There are fourteen plots divided between vegetables and flowers—from cabbages to zucchini, from cornflowers to primroses. There is always something blooming from mid-March to late November.

Pleasant Village Community Garden, 344–352 Pleasant Avenue, between 118th and 119th Streets. The wall painting of the Great Bear and Little Bear constellations includes the sun, moon, stars, and rain clouds. The mural is a result of children's programs that include storytelling, painting, and reading.

Jefferson Market Garden (opposite), at Greenwich Avenue between Sixth Avenue and West 10th Street. This twenty-three-year-old viewing garden, laid out by landscape designer Pamela Berdan, is now tended by Head Gardener Maggy Geiger and a number of volunteers. Brick paths wind through beds filled with flowering plants such as impatiens and abelia. The trees are yellow-woods circled with hostas.

The 91st Street Garden, in Riverside Park between 89th and 91st Streets. This garden of flowers and ornamental grasses on the esplanade was created in 1989, and continues to be maintained by The Garden People, Inc., a membership volunteer group that numbers about forty. It is a favorite of photographers and painters.

Front Yards and Backyards

Yards are a luxury, and really count in crowded cities like New York. Often there is only a small space in front of the house, and little sun in back. Designers are clever about using every inch of space and making gardens relatively care-free to accommodate busy lives. New plant materials that thrive in small, shady plots and make gardens green year round are giving city gardens new life and a new look.

On these pages: Three circles of brick paving create an interesting shape and unusual planting beds. Landscape architect Alice R. Ireys designed the backyard of Mr. and Mrs. Niels W. Johnsen's eighteenth-century brick townhouse on the Upper East Side of Manhattan. The Johnsens wanted a year-round green garden to view from their garden room. Now, American hollies, boxwood, and katsura trees are well established. The landscape firm that tends the garden, Holly Wood & Vine, brings in seasonal color with yellow and white bulbs in the spring, caladiums and white impatiens in the summer, and yellow chrysanthemums in the fall.

On the Park

The handsome Greek Revival house at 4 Gramercy Park West was built in 1837 by Alexander Jackson Davis and was home to Mayor James Harper from 1847 to 1869.

The present owners of number 4 are Alexander and Marine Zagoreos. In 1996, Marine Zagoreos redesigned the front garden, and Columbia Pictures, which used the house as a setting in the film *The Devil's Own,* arranged for the installation. Ivy and wisteria decorate the festive iron work. The urn and planting beds are filled with ivies, colorful geraniums, pansies, impatiens, and petunias. There are roses and a small hedge of clipped pachysandra, with junipers and euonymus adding texture.

A cottage garden on Fifth Avenue

The doorstep garden of this handsome Beaux-Arts townhouse on upper Fifth Avenue is green all year. Garden designer Bonnie Billet has the small space planted with boxwood hedges, evergreens, ferns, and a Japanese maple. She likes a formal yet lively look, with a good deal of variety. Color is added with seasonal plantings. For example, cyclamen in the fall, ornamental cabbages in winter, and yellow daffodils and tulips in the spring. The window boxes change often, to give pleasure to the owners and to passersby.

An Italian Garden

Many city backyards are challenging because of limited light and the lack of control over the background. In this small East Side garden, architect Dan Sherman solved the background problem by designing walls to control the view above the normal sight-line, and garden designer Galen Lee used plantings that would not create more shade.

The walls, which have a stucco finish sprayed over wood, are shaped and or-namented in an eighteenth-century Italianate garden style to complement the twentieth-century Italian-modern feel-ing of the house's interior. The formal, symmetrical plant-ing uses four columnar horn-beams, two on each side, with a weeping mulberry in the center arch. Korean box-wood trims the edges to give the garden its winter structure. The beds are planted with dwarf white azaleas and 'Thalia' narcissus. An auto-matic watering system keeps the space almost mainte-nance free. Only a glass wall separates the living area from the garden, so the own-ers can enjoy their green-and-white garden all year long.

A Federal Garden

The early nineteenth-century look of the architecture and furnishings of this East Side townhouse made garden designer Galen Lee think of trellising and symmetry. He completely enclosed the backyard with trellis painted an almost black green (sold as Schreuder Coach Green), and set it 4 inches away from an outside cedar fence painted white, so that the trellis casts fascinating shadow patterns as the light changes.

The owners wanted a garden to view year round. They also wanted it to be almost maintenance free, which it is, except for an annual clipping of the boxwood and the hollies. A pink flowering crab apple is regularly pruned to open the space to permit as much light as possible.

Dwarf hollies 'China girl' and 'China boy' insure berries. The trellis is home to a 'New Dawn' climbing rose, akebia vine, and clematis. In their season there are white azaleas, and for summer color, hybrid lilies in red, white, and pink. The nymph-and-dolphin fountain, made of English Coade stone (a composite), spills into a fiberglass faux-stone basin. These materials were chosen to avoid winter cracking. The brick floor is set in a herringbone pattern, the retaining wall is fieldstone. Planned for viewing and dining, the garden has become another room of the house.

A sunken garden in Neoclassical style

Walking up Fifth Avenue in the sixties, one's eyes are drawn to the handsome Romanesque–Renaissance mansion built for coal magnate Edward Berwind in 1896. It is one of the few remaining grand houses on Fifth Avenue across from Central Park. The architect cleverly planned an open space below street level to give the lower floor more light and air. Today, more than a hundred years later, the space looks like a Neoclassical garden in a romantic Roman ruin, owing to the ingenuity of fashion designer Adolfo Sardiña.

Adolfo sensed the magic of the place when the mansion was turned into cooperative apartments in the 1980s. And, while transforming a duplex apartment into a handsome background for his collection of fine portraits and French antiques, he began collecting stone figures and columns to create an entertaining view from his library.

Ornamental urns and planters of various sizes are filled with Boston and English ivy, and privet. The garden is kept very simply green for most of the year, but when chrysanthemums come onto the market, bright yellow ones are added for drama and to signal a change of season. Adolfo plants and tends the garden himself. Ivies and privet stand up surprisingly well to shifting winds and winter storms because of the garden's sheltered location. Passersby, curious to see what is below, are delighted to discover an enchanting garden beneath one of New York's busiest avenues.

Colonial Brazil in a New York garden

Flower designer Ronaldo Maia speaks of his East Side townhouse garden as his secret garden. And it is a surprise, for it is two floors off the ground. He wanted an extension of the house for entertaining, with the look and feel of a courtyard in the tropics. Maia realized his fantasy by adding a decorative balcony, plus a 15-foot-high trellis to the back wall to support the vines he brings back from his travels—moonflower, morning glory, honeysuckle, passionflower, and grape. The effect is dazzling.

The garden is an extension of the dining room. A rustic cedar table and chairs in the American Federal style help set the scene for dinners for six or buffet parties for twelve. The foliage whispers in the breeze and the water splashes in the fountain. The fountain itself, surrounded by climbing hydrangea, white oleander, and variegated ivy, is Italian; the white figure is Portuguese. Water recirculates in a terra-cotta tub.

The more weather-sensitive plants are moved inside for the cold months. An orange tree, planted by Maia's father some years ago, winters indoors as its reward for producing three or four edible fruits during the summer. This success is amazing, for the garden has only two hours of sun on a good day.

The growing process is started with a lightweight soil mixture and is further encouraged with fish emulsion and Zoodoo, a hippo manure Maia buys from the Missouri Botanical Garden in St. Louis. Plants thrive. The garden is mostly green, from dark to silvery tones, with white to lavender flowers. But there are exceptions, such as New Guinea impatiens with a bright flower and a dark leaf. All in all, the tangle of plants creates a most appealing setting for summer entertaining in the city.

A View of the Bay

The gardens of the Stanley Sorens' 1929 Tudor Revival house on Staten Island has breathtaking views of New York Bay and the Verrazano Bridge. When the Sorens moved in nearly thirty years ago, the garden was laid out with paths, trees, and shrubs—which garden designer Richard Iversen used as the bones of a new garden. Working with Marvin Davis of Romancing the Woods, a firm in Woodstock, New York, Iversen designed a rustic Gothic Revival–style gazebo of unbarked Eastern red cedar. It sits in just the right place for viewing Bay life. The plantings around it are mainly pink, silver, and blue, and include mandevilla vine, artemesia, sage, thyme, globe thistle, lavender, and peonies.

Wild with vines

Organic gardener and *Wall Street Journal* gardening columnist Patti Hagan seems to have solved many gardening problems in her Brooklyn backyard. She plants densely in water-retentive soil, and mulches heavily. She does not have weeds, and only if a plant looks stressed does she water, and then by hand. If there is a lot of rain, she may have to cut back the vines, but not too much, because they cover the chain-link fence and screen out the view of nearby buildings.

Hagan pushes seeds into pots and waits to see what happens. Her extravagance of vines includes four kinds of grapes, clematis, trumpet vine, cypress vine, porcelain berry, ivy, moonflower, honeysuckle, and wisteria. She plants for fragrance with gardenia, oleander, frangipani, jasmine, and Valencia oranges, among others. There is calico flower, and night-blooming cereus that is fragrant all night long. On the deck is Be-bop, a twelve-year-old foundling, one of seven cats that find the garden irresistible.

A garden in stone

Looking as if planted in a romantic ruin deep in the Italian countryside, this garden on Staten Island was created by Jacques Marchais (Mrs. Edna Klauber), the Asian art dealer and founder of the Museum of Tibetan Art next door. She designed the garden of her house as well as the Museum and its garden.

Collecting stones from all over the Island for the gifted Italian stonemason Primavano to work with, she laid out her garden on six terraced levels surrounded by a stone wall. The present owners, Richard and Lana Capuozzo, are preserving the original design and make sure that new plantings do not overshadow the stonework. Some of the ground covers are pachysandra, hostas, and English ivy. In spring there are tulips, azaleas, daffodils, and forsythia. In summer, white impatiens are added to all the green.

Overleaf: Another view of the Capuozzo garden

A garden of textures

Serenity and communion with nature were important to the owners of this townhouse garden. Responsible for both the interior and exterior, architects Tod Williams and Billie Tsien suggested that the garden be an extension of the rooms, rather than separate and purely decorative. The garden is on two levels, owing to the natural contours of the land, and the upper garden can be viewed from the family room, kitchen, and the living room above. There are many textures: a bridge made of stone and blue-green glass, white stucco walls, and American bluestone paving alternating with random insets of Mexican water-washed black stones. The planting materials follow the vertical and horizontal patterns of the enclosure. Timothy DuVal of Plant Specialists, Inc., specified 'Heritage' birches, tall and lacy, planted close together for a grove effect. Underneath, there is shade-tolerant liriope, European ginger, maidenhair fern, and cherry laurel. The bronze sculpture is Kiki Smith's *The Virgin Mary* of 1994.

Covered and cool

A charming old house in Brooklyn Heights with a wisteria-covered back porch is the oldest on the block, dating to about 1900. Now owned by Nicholas Callaway, it was the home of stage designer Oliver Smith for twenty years. Landscape architect Alice R. Ireys laid out a garden that is mostly green, with gingko, cypress, holly, pine trees, and evergreen shrubs. Just below the wisteria arbor, a fountain spills into a decorative catchment. The vine casts dappled shadows that are very welcome on a hot summer's day.

A carriage house court

In Manhattan's West 40s, amid 1870s tenement buildings, stands an 1820 carriage house whose courtyard garden is filled with greenery, cupids, and a fountain. Arthur Coppotelli's 30-by-20-foot courtyard garden is extremely sheltered, with some sun and relatively little temperature change, which encourages plants to thrive. Boston ivy covers the walls and the ground. An old rhododendron has spectacular pink blossoms in May. The floor is paved with slate. The Italian stone fountain dates from the 1920s.

A park at home

In 1977, Francis and Patricia Mason moved to one of the houses John Jacob Astor built in the 1850s on Morton Street in Greenwich Village. The yard was tremendously appealing, extending to 40 feet wide, unusual for a house only 17 feet wide. In the garden, designed by Patricia and landscape designer Pamela Berdan, and now in the care of horticulturist Mary Emma Harris, everything flourishes. There is an immense magnolia, a tall Leyland cypress, a Hinoke cypress, a cherry tree, and a gingko over 60 feet high. Coleus, sedum, begonias, caladiums, and corydalis border the lawn. The Mason garden opens to five other townhouse gardens, adding to the parklike feeling.

A perennial path

The spirit of an English country garden fills the backyard of an 1835 house on Staten Island. The present owners, Barnett Shepherd and Nick Dowen, keep the garden luxuriant with perennials. Sweet autumn clematis blooms on the arbor. Dwarf boxwood and Christmas ferns make the path very green, with black-eyed Susans adding color.

A Victorian feeling

David and Larry Marshall wanted lots of color and continuous bloom for the backyard of their Brooklyn shop, The Antique Room, which is part of their 1840s house. They asked Richard Iversen, garden designer and professor of horticulture, for a plan. Iversen rearranged existing plantings and brought in some older material to give the garden a mature look and a sense of history. There are French lilac trees, hollies, boxwood, redbud, dogwood, tree peonies, trumpet flowers, clematis, Asiatic lilies, Siberian iris, a variety of hydrangeas, and more. In the photograph, the center bed is ablaze with zinnias bordered with dwarf lavender. Under the guidance of landscaper Stan Murray, the garden is always evolving.

A learning garden

A green enclosure filled with nature is a great escape from the harshness of city streets. The garden at the Children's Storefront School in Harlem is that, and more. Classes are held in this joyous atmosphere, and studying and playing there is an adventure for young minds. Garden designer Keith Corlett used a mixture of hardy grasses to keep the yard green. Welcoming seats are placed here and there. To screen off the outside world, he used climbers on all the fences—roses, clematis, and silver lace vines. The beds are a combination of perennials and annuals such as black-eyed Susans, asters, day lilies, impatiens, and veronica. Although only 30 by 40 feet, the garden makes a delightful schoolyard.

More shade than sun

What to do with a town-house yard that has a scant three hours of sun a day? When Sally Bingham asked garden designer Keith Corlett to create a colorful garden in her backyard, the mature trees posed a problem. Fortunately, he was able to do some massive pruning to bring in more light. He then added a weeping beech that grows down rather than out, and concentrated on shade-loving plants such as hostas and ferns (mainly ostrich and maidenhair ferns).

Annuals in vivid colors are brought in each season, along with tropical plants, like palms and mandevilla vines, which are not expected to last beyond the warm summer months. Garden furniture and two wooden obelisks are painted a sky blue that changes color as the light changes. Despite the lack of sun, the garden seems to vibrate with color. To decorate the fence and to make the space even more entertaining, Corlett designed plaques of eight mythological goddesses, and with wit and charm he included a likeness of the owner.

The English touch

Mr. and Mrs. Richard E. Diamond's Staten Island backyard is filled with ideas and plants brought back from their travels. The checkerboard garden, one of six sitting areas, is made of grass and pea gravel. It was copied from a photograph of an English garden. The terra-cotta pot man is similar to one who stands in front of a London flower shop. He has marigolds in his basket and ferns on his head, and always carries a flag on the Fourth of July.

Designed to be natural

A garden to view from indoors, and step out to, perhaps with the sound of a fountain to offset the din of the East River Drive, was what the owner had in mind. She called in the firm of Oehme, van Sweden & Associates, who created a walled green garden with stone boulders and limestone shelves of cascading water. The walls are covered with silver lace, clematis, and wisteria vines, and espaliered euonymus and climbing hydrangea. There are specimen dogwoods and magnolia trees, and evergreen ground covers. With many textures and subtle color changes, something is always blooming.

A garden off the kitchen, where one can dine every night if the weather permits, is a source of joy. That is what Margaret and Ken Leung have created in the Park Slope landmarked district of Brooklyn. The house, dated 1899, was designed by the architect Montrose W. Morris. The property particularly appealed to the Leungs because, while the main part of the garden faces south for sun-loving flowers, there is also a shade garden. Stories of a golden fountain in the garden's early life were intriguing, and digging revealed water pipes at the spot bricked over for the dining table.

The garden is a family affair. He tends the grass and she tends the flowers, both under the watchful eye of J. Michael Sokasits of Gardenscape, Inc. Virginia creeper, climbing hydrangea, and wisteria have made themselves at home against the neighbor's wall. Birch trees ripple in the breeze. Raised beds contain such plantings as rhododendrons and hostas. The giant terra-cotta pots with their tall metal frames encourage roses, clematis, ivies, and various annuals. It is a garden with a history that is perfect now for the Leung's way of living.

A family garden

Three on a block

A row of turn-of-the-century white limestone houses in Brooklyn sports cheerful front-yard gardens. Ron, Regina, and Brendan Mysliwiec concentrate on roses. Jeri Hansen uses a variety of plants, with miniature evergreens in stone planters. Nancy Lunsford sometimes plants corn. These three small gardens make a big impression.

Dining Terraces

W_{hy} is eating outdoors always such an adventure? It can be a hot dog from a street vendor, a gala lunch under a tent, or a family barbecue under the stars. Whatever, with it comes that great feeling of freedom, change. Restaurants and cafés are spilling out onto sidewalks and opening gardens to catch the breeze—never mind air conditioning. At home, tables, chairs, and containers filled with flowers and greenery are appearing in all sorts of arrangements on rooftops and in backyards. The rush to eating outdoors is on.

Preceding pages: A corner of Pamela Scurry's rooftop terrace

A Victorian rooftop

There is a penthouse terrace on upper Fifth Avenue, overlooking the Central Park Reservoir, that has all the charm of an English cottage garden. This is exactly what Pamela Scurry had in mind when the family moved into the apartment twenty-three years ago, and, since she is the gardener, there was no question that she would have the romantic garden she wanted.

Victoriana is very much a part of Pamela Scurry's life, at home and in her Madison Avenue shop, The Wicker Garden. A Victorian-style greenhouse, extending the master bedroom of the apartment onto the terrace, is always filled with greenery. (A bathtub in its center is a good plant container when there is a party.) Victorian wrought-iron furniture is scattered about the terrace, along with a great mix of flowering plants. There are several maples and a mimosa tree. Her plant palette is mainly pink, blue, and laven-der. Containers spill over with roses, English geraniums, miniature hydrangea bushes, cascading petunias, snapdragons, delphiniums, foxgloves, and forget-me-nots. Ivy, clematis, and mandevilla on walls and lattices make a colorful background. The Scurrys love to eat on the terrace and often entertain with teas and brunches. At night, strings of lights and the city's glow make the terrace an enchanted place for supper parties.

The owners of this Upper East Side townhouse treat the third-floor terrace and the living room as one. The Ellery Gordons like the idea of a

Margorie Reed Gordon, a private dealer in antique Venetian glass and author of the Preface to *Venetian Glass: Confections in Glass*

A living terrace

living room without borders, and have filled it with outdoor artifacts such as a terrarium, a stone caryatid, a bark chair, and garden statuary. On the terrace, the cedar sectional seating is arranged traditionally, with planters worked into the design. It is a box garden that encourages climbing hydrangeas, clematis, and a number of annuals. One is also apt to see petunias, impatiens, cosmos, ageratum, dusty miller, foxglove, and lupine.

1855–1914 (Harry N. Abrams, Inc., 1998), lunches on the terrace almost every summer day. She calls it a joyous spot. Ellery Gordon is a good cook, so they entertain with frequent barbecues as well as a cocktail party to open and one to close the summer season. The terrace–living room combination allows guests to move indoors and out with pleasure and ease.

Colorful entertaining

Imaginative design and a large variety of plantings make this second-floor terrace a very colorful place for summer dining. The terrace belongs to David and Larry Marshall, who own The Antique Room, a popular shop in Brooklyn that specializes in Victorian decorative arts from 1820 to 1890. The Marshalls supplied the furniture for the film *The Age of Innocence*.

Landscaper Stan Murray has filled containers and pots with such plants as vivid red coleus, a collection of begonias including a vibrant Rex begonia, 'Mr. Lincoln' and 'Ferdinand Pickard' roses, butterfly bush, miscanthus, hibiscus, banana trees, and the beautiful golden chalice vine. The pergola is covered with a very lush wisteria. Barbecue parties are a great success in this semitropical atmosphere.

A skyline view

When Timothy and Dagny DuVal bought an old paint and varnish factory in Long Island City some years ago, they wanted to have a guest apartment and a garden on the roof. Now, both have been accomplished. The 1880s building accommodates their own living quarters, offices for their garden design firm, Plant Specialists, Inc., and fifteen other tenants ranging from a baker to a furniture maker.

Dagny DuVal designed, planted, and continues to maintain the roof garden. Old timbers found in the building were used to make the pergola that shelters the dining area. The other section is left open to enjoy the dramatic views of the Queensboro Bridge and the Manhattan skyline. Casual suppers, with the city lights at night a blaze of diamonds, are based on food cooked on the grill. Weekend lunches take advantage of the sun and the breezes from the East River.

A mixture of dwarf and regular black pines and an assortment of grasses that includes pennisetum create a background for the garden.

Loosestrife, one of the weeds that grow year round in the wetlands of New York, thrives in this unusual setting, with purply-pink blooms midsummer. Breynia, with its variegated white-and-pink leaf, is a tropical plant sent up from Florida every spring that likes this sunny rooftop. A lot of color is provided by a profusion of 'Betty Prior' roses, and ivy has been started, with hopes it will eventually cover all the walls. Like most gardens, it is a work in progress. Cast pebbled pavers were chosen to reflect the light, and the large planters

are wood or terra cotta. Black plastic growing pots, spilling over with blooms, are often massed together for an extravagant display of color. The flowers hide the sides of these lightweight containers, which are easily moved around. There is an automatic drip watering system, and small, low-voltage fixtures light the plantings from above and below. The garden has a life of its own, and is so appealing that the DuVals no longer feel they have to escape to the country on weekends.

A
room
in the
sky

A large flat roof with a high protecting wall was the dreary view for an Upper East Side apartment. The owners, Mr. and Mrs. Sam Silber, decided something could be done about it, and called in landscape architect David Varnell of Kelly/Varnell, Inc.

They liked Varnell's idea of creating an "outdoor room" by closing in a relatively small area of the rooftop and elevating part of it to make the view accessible. The parapet wall is eight feet high, so the cedarwood structure was designed on three levels. The feeling of a European garden—perhaps in Tuscany—comes to mind. A pergola and a hardy purple wisteria give shade. Among the plantings are climbing hydrangea, Boston ivy, Virginia creeper, inkberry, periwinkle, liriope, catnip, white birch trees—all selected to retain a sense of openness. The very decorative cupid is a find brought home from a French flea market. Springtime parties held from six to half-past eight catch the great downtown views and spectacular sunsets.

Dining in a bamboo glade

Finding an exotic bamboo garden behind an old brownstone townhouse on the Upper East Side of New York City seems unlikely. But, indeed there is one, and it is evergreen with a luxuriant stand of bamboo in full leaf all year long. Interior designer Contessa Muriel Brandolini d'Adda's luscious, jungly green garden is a dramatic extension of rooms filled with brilliant colors and patterns from the East. Her heritage is Vietnamese, Venezuelan, and French, and she brings stylish elements of these cultures together here. For the idea of the garden, she credits Jean Laffont, whose own beautiful gardens in Paris and the South of France are much admired.

Created in the summer of 1995 by Timothy DuVal of Plant Specialists, Inc., it was an almost instant garden. Special beds built with barriers to protect the roots of neighbors' ginkgo trees were prepared for *Pseudosasa japonica*, a bamboo that tolerates shade, and when planted already stood 10 to 12 feet high. The walls of green leaves make the space a dramatic yet very private setting for entertaining family and friends. The table in the charming bamboo pavilion seats six, and as many as forty have dined at a series of round tables covered with colorful Indian cottons.

This Upper East Side apartment offers more than just rooms with a view. The wraparound terrace appealed to Edith and Hamilton Kean when they bought their penthouse several years ago. She is a landscape designer for GreenThumb, New York City's community garden program, and serves on the boards of The Horticultural Society of New York and The New York Botanical Garden. Gardening is not just a passing fancy for the Keans.

Dining on the river

There is a sheltered space for dining outdoors on the terrace, and a solarium for dining indoors. The Keans enjoy their terrace garden and the spectacular view of the East River and Long Island Sound year round. Working with horticulturist Donald Henley, Edith Kean greatly expanded the design and plantings on the terrace. One inherited treasure is a Japanese black pine that stands in the most exposed corner (see pages 2–3). It is at least twenty-five years old, and is carefully candled and pruned each year. Other trees include river birch, Higon cherry, and a limber pine that does particularly well on windy terraces. Plantings that like this terrace are numerous. They include a blueberry bush, purple liatris, fothergilla, robinia, salvia, Russian sage, and Hakonechloa grass. Containers of seasonal flowers can be moved about. The pots photographed here are spilling over with petunias, fuchsias, and pennisetum. Like all good gardens, this terrace has a life of its own, with a changing scene of contrasting greens and colorful flowering plants.

Outdoor evenings

Creative terrace plantings can work magic for a city apartment. This terrace, off a rooftop study on upper Park Avenue, is an example. The owners, the Stephen R. Colens, wanted the homey feeling and the fragrance of a country garden. Landscape architect Dan Stewart created the original plan, and recently Plant Specialists, Inc., completed a refurbishing. The bones of the garden consist of stone-colored wooden planters extending the color of the building, and large stone pots placed to highlight the decorative balustrade. Evergreens screen off certain sightlines. Vines and perennials were chosen for fragrance, for flowering throughout the summer, and for autumn color. The ornamental grass in the stone pots is miscanthus, which moves gracefully in the wind. The plantings catch the light and the breeze, making the terrace a delightful place to be. The Colens sometimes breakfast there, but particularly like it for cocktails, or for dessert, when they can enjoy the moon, the stars, and the panorama of Central Park.

room, salmon-colored ones outside the dining room painted a delicious salmon color. Off-white fiberglass boxes in the classic Versailles style—high and low, wide and narrow—were arranged along the walls.

The plantings include young, pruned weeping willows, delicate-leaf Japanese maples, espaliered apple trees, hydrangeas, cotoneasters, fancy leaf geraniums, and fuchsia, with heliotrope for scent and color. A nineteenth-century marble figure placed on the terrace opposite the living room entrance draws the eye outdoors. A small grove of Kwanzan cherries will soon create a decorative arch over the figure. On summer evenings, at supper parties for six or eight, guests enjoy the sunset and their magical surroundings.

An English garden in New York

When the owner of this penthouse first moved in, she asked New York garden designer Renny Reynolds to create an instant garden that would look fresh and sparkling in time for her first party.

Using mature plants in movable boxes and pots,

Reynolds captured the natural look of an English garden. To complement the inside rooms created by interior designer Anthony Mallen, he chose a garden palette of soft blue, pink, lavender, and white. With charm and whimsy, lavender climbing roses were planted outside a blue bed-

A townhouse terrace

The look and feel of the south of France is what floral designer Olivier Guini wanted for the dining terrace he created at the New York designer showhouse benefitting the American Hospital in Paris. The brick paving, the fantasy trellis on the back wall, and the lacy locust trees were already in place when he began his work. To remind one of the wines of France, and to keep the symmetry and a formal feeling, he added a series of handsome terracotta planters filled with tall stands of grapevine. The ground cover is baby's-tears. Sunflowers and olive branches, another French touch, are in a recessed planter in the tabletop made of lava stone. Guini thinks this volcanic material, which can be enameled in any color, is today's new marble. Certainly, the look of the table and its setting are most inviting.

Overleaf:

Western panorama

This terrace, off a sixteenth-floor penthouse in Greenwich Village, faces the Hudson River. Its owner, Ivan Schneider, wanted nothing to interfere with the panorama of rooftops and river, so he asked garden designer Jeff Mendoza for a plan using very few trees.

Mendoza brought in lightweight, weather-resistant containers made of galvanized sheet metal. A see-through railing of metal and glass gives the terrace an open feeling.

Light and airy plantings, such as variegated fountain grass, catch the breezes from the west. There are two Irish junipers, and a young Japanese maple. Underplantings are mixed perennials and annuals in pastel pinks, mauves, and white. The apartment, with floor-to-ceiling windows, opens to this delightful terrace garden, in which the owner breakfasts on summer mornings and entertains in the evenings.

Botanical Gardens

Great institutions are working to save the natural environment through research and education. Five such organizations are included here. Large or small, each is remarkable in its own way. Their scientists, scholars, and educators explain what nature does for us and what we can do to preserve it. Their gardeners and designers create beautiful landscapes and gardens that offer fresh ideas and give great pleasure.

The New York Botanical Garden

One of the world's great research and teaching institutions, The New York Botanical Garden conducts its work on 250 acres in the borough of the Bronx and in many far-flung places throughout the world. The largest collection of preserved plant specimens in this hemisphere is housed in the garden's herbarium, and its library of botanical and horticultural literature is renowned.

This extraordinary organization was founded in 1891, with a board of notables—Cornelius Vanderbilt as president, Andrew Carnegie as vice-president, J. P. Morgan as treasurer, and Nathaniel Lord Britton, a botanist and professor at Columbia University, as treasurer and first director. Architect Calvert Vaux, who worked with Frederick Law Olmsted on the de-

sign of Central Park, was asked to make a landscape plan. Vaux's work was the foundation for the garden's layout by Britton, Columbia colleague Lucien Underwood, gardener Samuel Hanshaw, and civil engineer John Brinley. Their respect for the magnificent natural terrain—the Bronx River, wetlands, ponds, and a virgin forest—is still evident.

Twenty-eight outdoor gardens and plant collections amaze, delight, and instruct visitors and gardening students throughout the seasons. Basic and advanced gardening courses, gardening demonstrations, walking and tram tours, and plant sales are among the activities that fill the calendar. To visit The New York Botanical Garden is to walk into a world of natural wonders.

The Rock Garden

On the preceding pages: Built on 2.5 acres, rock-loving plants gathered from the mountains, woodlands, and meadows of America and on botanical expeditions to almost every continent demonstrate an astonishing variety and beauty. The garden was designed and built almost sixty years ago by T. H. Everett, the Director of Horticulture. The curator is Robert Bartolomei.

The seasonal borders

A double-bordered walk leading to the Enid A. Haupt Conservatory (below and opposite) blazes with tulips, annuals, and chrysanthemums in their seasons. The collection of 17,600 tulips of 70 different cultivars is considered an important "reference library." In summer, these border gardens are filled with more than 100 varieties of annuals, and in the fall, with brilliant drifts of chrysanthemums.

The Enid A. Haupt Conservatory

This resplendent structure, opened in 1902, was patterned after the Crystal Palace, built for the 1851 Great Exhibition in London. The conservatory, restored in 1997 by the garden staff and renowned architect John Belle of Byer, Blinder, Belle is the setting for an ecotour around the world. Landscape architect Jon Charles Coe and garden curators have created lush displays of living plants from the tropical lowland and upland rain forests and from the deserts of Africa and the Americas. There is an aquatic plant gallery with papyrus specimens, and a collection of climbers—twiners, scramblers, and creepers. The greenhouse collection of the palms of the Americas is the most extensive in the world under glass. Other special collections include subtropical plants, hanging gardens, and seasonal exhibitions. Joseph Kerwin is Director and Francisca Coehlo is Curator of the Conservatory.

The Peggy Rockefeller Rose Garden

The rose, flower of love and celebration, is glorified in this garden. Much-admired landscape architect Beatrix Jones Farrand originally designed the garden in 1916, but it was not completed to her specifications until its reconstruction in 1987. Eighty-three beds, along three walkways, radiate from a large gazebo almost smothered in the lush blooms that climb the decorative frames encircling it. The garden's rosarians, directed by Michael Ruggiero, are always evaluating various types of roses, and plant only varieties available to home gardeners. More than 200 kinds of old roses and modern roses are grown here.

The Jane Watson Irwin Perennial Garden

Designed in the "natural" style that became popular in England early in the twentieth century, this garden has all the charm one expects from such a garden. The luxurious drifts of color and texture that look so carefree have, in fact, been carefully orchestrated by public garden designer Lynden B. Miller. Primarily planted in herbaceous perennials—those sturdy herblike, nonwoody plants that send up new growth each year—the garden also includes some trees, shrubs, annuals, and biennials. This mixed border combination contributes to the garden's structure and to its exuberant display throughout the growing season.

The garden is divided into six sections: cool, hot, shade, and bog sections, plus a fall room for autumn plantings and a vine collection. Photographed here are beds planted with cool colors: varieties include hellebores, Japanese anemones, salvia, sedum, hydrangeas, and asters. The clipped hedge is yew. The gardener in charge is Elizabeth Invar.

The Nancy Bryan Luce Herb Garden

Some of the most attractive early gardens were the parterres in the cloisters of the Renaissance monasteries. They were peaceful places for meditation, and they were practical, filled with plants used in cooking, medicines, perfumes, and dyes.

Herbs are perennials that lack woody structures above ground, die back in winter, and return in spring. Some woody plants are also considered herbs, such as lavender, thyme, and rosemary. Herbs have their ornamental side, giving a garden color and texture.

This garden was established in 1948 by the New York Unit of the Herb Society of America. In 1991, it was replanned by English landscape designer Penelope Hobhouse, who is known for her romantic garden designs. In borders, and in beds in a double-knot pattern of clipped boxwood, she arranged ninety-two different European and American herbs in decorative profusion. Lisa Cady is the gardener.

Wave Hill

Wave Hill sits high above the Hudson River, in the Riverdale section of the Bronx. On this twenty-eight-acre estate, one can learn about horticulture, the environment, land management, landscape history, and the visual and performing arts.

The property has an interesting history. Wave Hill House was built in 1843 for jurist William Lewis Morris. In 1866 it was bought by publisher William Henry Appleton, who added a garden and greenhouses and entertained pioneering natural scientists such as Thomas Henry Huxley and Charles Darwin. In 1903, financier George W. Perkins purchased the estate and joined it to others he owned along the river. Perkins expanded the gardens, planting rare trees and shrubs in harmony with the natural landscape. The Perkins-Freeman family deeded Wave Hill to New York City in 1960.

Five years later, a nonprofit corporation was formed to help support its mission to study and demonstrate the interaction between people and the natural world.

Wave Hill, a National Environmental Landmark, consists of eighteen landscaped gardens, ten woodland and native habitats, four historic buildings, and five greenhouses. In the horticultural collections are 1,200 genera, 3,250 species. With all of this, it still retains many of its unique qualities as a private estate. According to Marco Polo Stufano, Director of Horticulture, the gardens are designed to be small and approachable rather than grand and institutional. Each has

nooks, corners, and segments with ideas for the home gardener.

The Wild Garden (opposite page, above) has plants from all over the world, in what appears to be a natural profusion. It was inspired by William Robinson, an influential nineteenth-century English garden designer. During their seasons there are Lenten roses, snowdrops, crocuses, daffodils, poppies, clematis, Scotch thistle, and salvia. Great, green mounds of yew, brilliant red amaranthus, and orangy cut-leaf staghorn sumac give the garden spectacular color.

The Flower Garden (opposite page, below) is an old-fashioned cottage garden

with rustic fences and brick pathways. It is filled with radiant color from early spring to late autumn—flowering jasmine, bleeding heart, peonies, roses, hydrangeas, and dahlias.

The Pergola (above), typical of those found in an Italian garden, offers a glorious view of the Palisades on the New Jersey side of the Hudson River. This traditional garden structure is a place for climbing vines and clusters of terra-cotta pots filled with tropical and semitropical plants. Coleus, acalypha, cuphea, and thunbergia, in the colors of autumn foliage, are varieties to be found here.

The Staten Island Botanical Garden

Eighty-three acres on the north shore of Staten Island contain a remarkable botanical garden. It began as an arboretum in 1960, started by citizens who remembered the island when it was resplendent with farms and forests. The current name was legally adopted in 1973, and in 1977 the city provided land at Snug Harbor Cultural Center for a permanent botanical garden.

Forty-one acres of designed gardens include the Heritage Rose Garden, Pond Garden, Herb Garden, Lions' Sensory Garden for the Disabled, Butterfly Garden, Potager Garden, and a Chinese Scholar's Garden created by artisans from China. There are Victorian parterres, an allee, and over 2,000 specimen trees and shrubs in a landscape collection. Woodlands, meadows, and wet-

lands are home to rare flora and fauna.

The planting list for the White Garden, shown here, includes nearly a hundred different varieties, such as hollyhocks, windflower, columbine, bellflower, turtlehead, Japanese painted fern, sea holly, foamflower, Adam's-needle, pearlbush, hardy kiwi, Virgin's bower, and fleece plant. The garden, designed by horticulturist Gregory Lord, is bounded by Roger Sherry's decorative white trellis enclosure.

The English Perennial Garden is patterned after the exuberant border gardens of England. The north border was designed by Gregory Lord, the other three by Richard Iversen. Their planting lists include Nippon daisies, oriental poppies, black-eyed Susan, Culver's root, and Mexican Hat. These lush borders are full of ideas for home gardeners.

The Queens Botanical Garden

Started as a horticultural exhibit at the 1939 New York World's Fair, this amazing institution now features five teaching collections—bee, bird, woodland, herb, and a pinetum. There are six backyard demonstration gardens, a wedding garden, an arboretum.

The Queens Botanical Garden Society was formed in 1946, and, picking up from where the World's Fair left off, developed a showcase for horticulture in New York City's largest borough. The garden flourished, and in 1960 was moved to its present 39-acre site in the northwest corner of Flushing Meadows Corona Park. It opened to the public in 1963.

A recently added display garden, designed by staff horticulturist Patricia Cook, is devoted to perennials. Beds of hot and cool colors play against each other. For example, rudbeckia, heliopsis, and helenium, in contrast to alchemilla, phlox, and artemisia. This is a garden of plants that thrive in the moist conditions of Queens, and was planned to help local residents with their own gardening.

A delightful herb garden, designed with formal box-wood beds, displays herbs according to use. Culinary herbs include lovage, dill, and coriander. Some of the medicinal herbs are comfrey, chamomile, and valerian. Mint, lavender, and eucalyptus are among the herbs used in various crafts. Geraniums and lemon balm are among the aromatic herbs.

The Wedding Garden, in Victorian style, has a decorative gazebo and a bridge that crosses a bubbling brook. The borders are brilliant with salvia, celosia, canna, fox-glove, and snapdragon. Trees include flowering cherries and crab apples.

The Brooklyn Botanic Garden

One of the most beautiful botanic gardens in the world is in Brooklyn. The idea of the garden was conceived by civic leaders in 1892, six years before the city of Brooklyn became a borough of the greater city of New York. In 1910, the garden came to life on land still strewn with boulders from the Ice Age. Philanthropist Alfred T. White raised funds for the project, and the renowned architectural firm of McKim, Mead & White designed the administration building and the Palm House. This was an early success story in environmental restoration as the property had previously been a dumping ground for building rubble.

Now, on fifty-two acres adjacent to the Brooklyn Museum of Art, this internationally respected research and educational institution is teaching the art of gardening.

A series of display gardens act as outdoor classrooms, among them gardens of roses, fragrance, herbs, flora native to the New York area, and rock plants. There are special collections of conifers, daffodils, Oriental flowering cherries, lilacs, magnolias, and water lilies, all arranged to give pleasure as they teach. A children's gardening project has functioned since 1914. The Steinhardt Conservatory, designed by Davis, Brody & Associates, was opened in 1988. It re-creates desert and tropical plant habitats from around the world in a series of amazing glasshouses.

Cherry Esplanade (left) is ablaze with 'Kwanzan' cherries against a background of Norway maples.

Cherry Walk (below) is a romantic bower of forty varieties of Japanese flowering cherries.

Japanese Hill-and-Pond Garden

The garden as a sacred place, a place to be at one with the universe, has been part of Japanese culture for centuries. In the Hill-and-Pond Garden, opened in 1915, landscape architect Takeo Shiota placed meaningful elements such as a viewing pavilion, stone lanterns and shrines, and a red torii gate. It is said that he did not approve the arrangement of the waterfall until the music of the cascading water was to his liking. Through the years, trees and shrubs have been shaped with careful pruning.

Now a mature garden of great beauty, it is in the care of horticulturist Doug Dudgeon. Among the trees are Japanese maple 'Burgundy Lace', Japanese cherries 'Shirotae' and 'Taki-Nioi', and Yoshino cherry.

Lily Pool Terrace displays a hundred varieties of hardy and tropical water lilies in two rectangular pools. An elegant heron often surveys the colorful scene. Some of the plants photographed here are sacred lotus 'Carolina Snow' and 'Perry's Giant Sunburst', and hardy water lilies 'James Brydon,' 'Albatross,' 'Rose Nymph,' and 'Lemon Scent'.

The collection is managed by horticulturist Cynthia Giancaspro.

The Cranford Rose Garden was designed by landscape architect Harold Caparn in 1927. His plan was both formal and practical. To give the garden shape and a presence year round, he enclosed the space in decorative white trellis fencing with a viewing pavilion at one end. He used panels of green lawn to separate three rows of planting beds and give them a sense of order, then edged the garden in brick paths covered with arches for climbing roses. The result is a framework for a glorious rose garden.

Managed by Stephen Scanniello, a noted rosarian and author of numerous books on growing roses, the Cranford Rose Garden has an international reputation. Its vast collection includes some 5,000 rose bushes of nearly 1,200 varieties. Seen here is the pavilion covered with 'Dr. W. Van Fleet,' 'Handel' and 'Penelope'. In and around the bird bath are 'The Doctor' and 'American Beauty.' From late May to early December, the garden is filled with color and fragrance.

Following pages: A weeping Higan cherry in the Japanese Hill-and-Pond Garden at the Brooklyn Botanic Garden

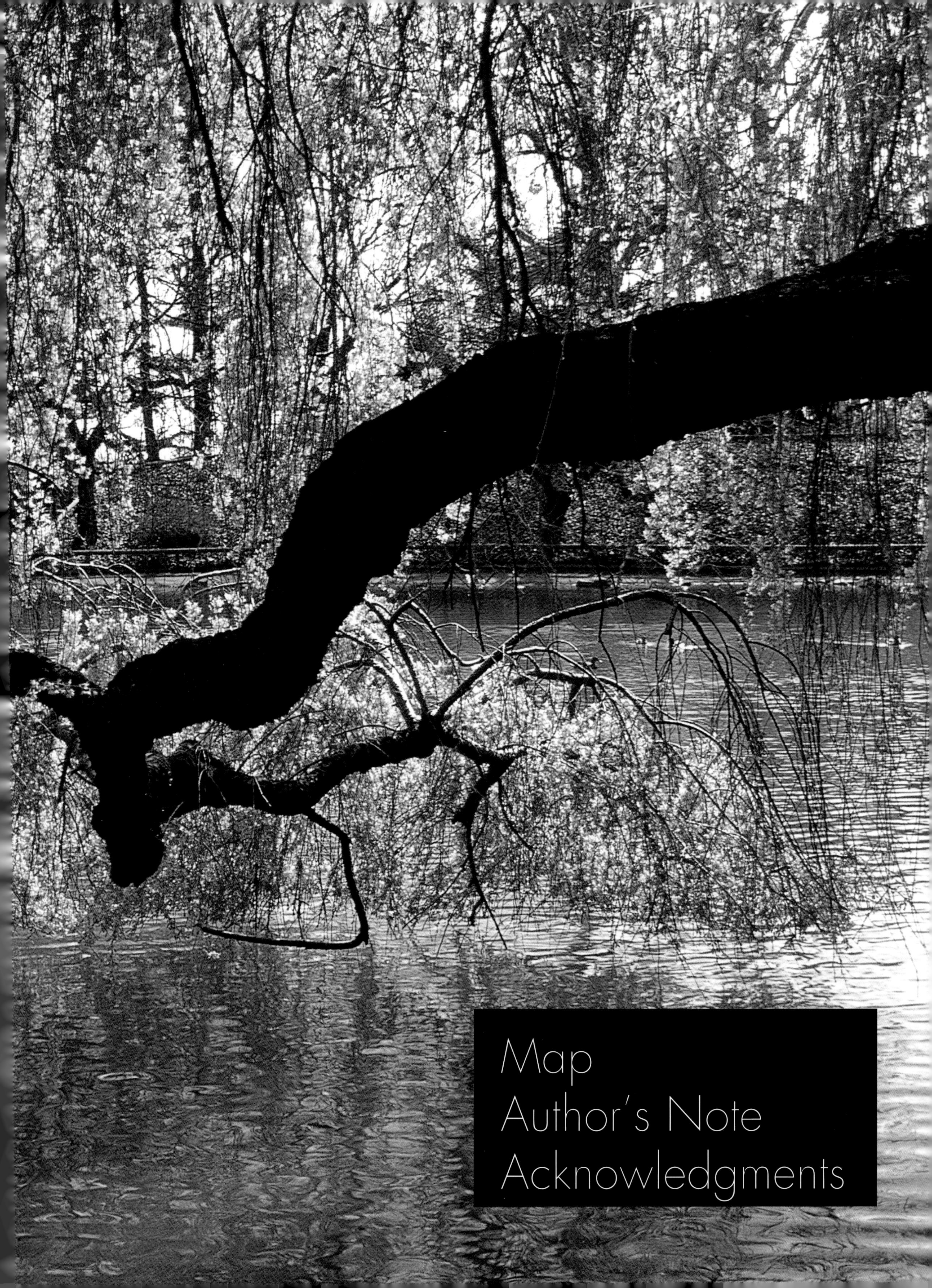

Map
Author's Note
Acknowledgments

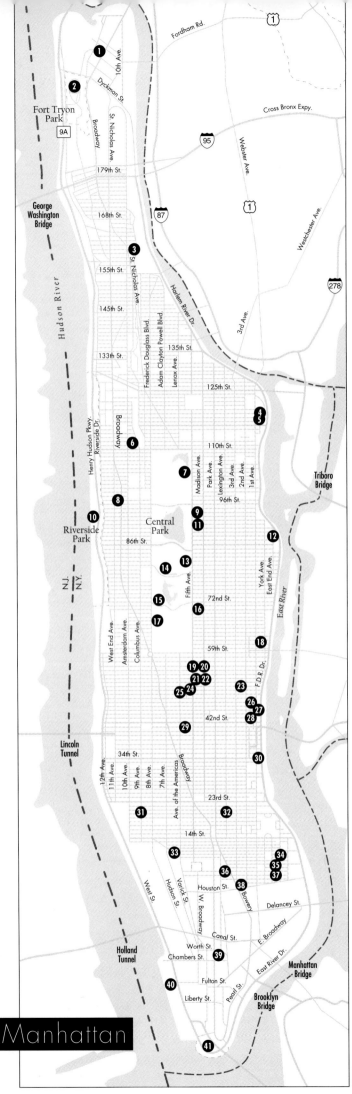

New York City Gardens Open to the Public

Many of the gardens shown in this book are open to the public and can be enjoyed year round. Their locations are indicated by number on the maps shown here, and listed both alphabetically and numerically.

A Visitors should telephone for hours that gardens are open
B Days and hours are posted on signs
C Can be entered or seen as one passes by
  All gardens in Manhattan unless otherwise noted

Abigail Adams Smith Museum, 18 A
421 East 61st Street
(212) 838-6878

Bartow–Pell Mansion Museum, 42 A
895 Shore Road, Pelham Bay Park, Bronx
(718) 885-1461

Battery Park City, 41 C
Between Battery Place, State Street and the Hudson River

Brisas la Caribe, 37 B
237 East 3rd Street

Brooklyn Botanic Garden, 48 A
1000 Washington Avenue, Brooklyn
(718) 622-4433

Bryant Park, 29 C
Between 5th and 6th Avenues and 40th and 42nd Streets

Carlton Garden, 47 B
Carlton Street, between Fulton and Green Streets, Brooklyn

Cathedral of St. John the Divine, 6 A
1047 Amsterdam Avenue at 112th Street
(212) 316-7540

Channel Gardens at Rockefeller Center, 24 C
5th Avenue between 50th and 51st Streets

Cloisters, The 2 A
193rd Street & Fort Washington Avenue, Fort Tryon Park
(212) 923-3700

Conservatory Garden, Central Park, 7 A
Fifth Avenue & 105th Street
(212) 360-2766

Cooper–Hewitt National Design Museum, 11 A
Smithsonian Institution, 2 East 91st Street
(212) 849-8300

Dyckman Farmhouse Museum, 1 A
4881 Broadway at 204th Street
(212) 304-9422

Federal Plaza, 39 C
Broadway between Worth & Duane Streets

Ford Foundation, 28 A
320 East 43rd Street
(212) 573-5000

Frick Collection, 16 A
1 East 70th Street
(212) 288-0700

General Theological Seminary of the Episcopal Church, 31 A
175 Ninth Avenue, between 20th and 21st Streets
(212) 243-5150

Gracie Mansion Conservancy, 12 A
East End Avenue at 88th Street
(212) 570-4751

Gramercy Park, 32 C
Between 20th and 21st Streets, between Lexington Avenue & Irving Place

Greenacre Park, 23 B
221 East 51st Street

Holy Rosary Garden, 4 B
119th Street, between Pleasant and 1st Avenues

Jacques Marchais Museum of Tibetan Art, 50 A
338 Lighthouse Avenue, Staten Island
(718) 987-3500

Japan Society, 26 A
333 East 47th Street
(212) 832-1155

Jefferson Market Garden, 33 B
Greenwich Avenue, between 6th Avenue and West 10th Street

Liz Christie Garden, 38 B
Bowery and Houston Street

Lotus Garden, 8 B
West 97th Street between Broadway and West End

Merchant's House Museum, 36 A
29 East 4th Street
(212) 777-1089

Metropolitan Museum of Art, 13 A
1000 5th Avenue at 82nd Street
(212) 535-7710

Morris–Jumel Mansion Museum, 3 A
65 Jumel Terrace at 160th Street
(212) 923-8008

Museum of Modern Art, 21 A
11 West 53rd Street
(212) 708-9400

New York Botanical Garden, 44 A
200th Street and Southern Blvd., Bronx
(718) 817-8700

91st Street Garden, Riverside Park, 10 B
Between 89th and 91st Streets

9th Street Community Garden and Park, 34 B
9th Street and Avenue C

Isamu Noguchi Garden Museum, 46 A
33-37 Vernon Blvd., Long Island City, Queens
(718) 545-8842

Paley Park, 22 B
1 East 53rd Street

Pleasant Village Community Garden, 5 B
344-352 Pleasant Avenue, between 118th and 119th Streets

Queens Botanical Garden, 45 A
43-50 Main Street, Flushing, Queens
(718) 886-3800

Ramakrishna–Vivekananda Center, 9 C
17 East 94th Street

Howard A. Rusk Institute of Rehabilitation Medicine, 30 A
400 East 34th Street
(212) 263-6058

Sculpture Garden at 590 Madison Ave., 20 C
Madison Ave. at 56th Street

Shakespeare Garden, Central Park, 14 C
79th Street and West Drive in the Park

6 B–C Community Garden, 35 B
624 East 6th Street

Staten Island Botanical Garden, 49 A
1000 Richmond Terrace, Staten Island
(718) 273-8200

Stephens–Prier House at Historic Richmond Town, 51 A
249 Center Street, Staten Island
(718) 351-1617

Strawberry Fields, Central Park, 16 C
Central Park West at 72nd Street

Tavern on the Green, Central Park, 17
Central Park at 67th Street
Open to the public for dining only

Trump Tower Trees, 19 C
5th Avenue at 56th Street

1251 Avenue of the Americas, 25 C
Between 49 and 50th Streets

United Nations Garden, 27 C
1st Avenue at 47th Street

Wave Hill, 43 A
675 West 252nd Street, Riverdale, Bronx
(718) 549-3200

Winter Garden at World Financial Center, 40 C
West Street between Liberty and Vesey Streets

1 A
Dyckman Farmhouse Museum
4881 Broadway at 204th Street
(212) 304-9422

2 A
The Cloisters
193rd Street & Fort Washington Avenue, Fort
Tryon Park
(212) 923-3700

3 A
Morris–Jumel Mansion Museum
65 Jumel Terrace at 160th Street
(212) 923-8008

4 B
Holy Rosary Garden
119th Street, between Pleasant and 1st Avenues

5 B
Pleasant Village Community Garden
344-352 Pleasant Avenue, between 118th
and 119th Streets

6 A
Cathedral of St. John the Divine
1047 Amsterdam Avenue at 112th Street
(212) 316-7540

7 A
Conservatory Garden
Central Park
Fifth Avenue & 105th Street
(212) 360-2766

8 B
Lotus Garden
West 97th Street between Broadway and
West End

9 C
Ramakrishna–Vivekananda Center
17 East 94th Street

10 B
91st Street Garden, Riverside Park
Between 89th and 91st Streets

11 A
Cooper–Hewitt National Design Museum
Smithsonian Institution, 2 East 91st Street
(212) 849-8300

12 A
Gracie Mansion Conservancy
East End Avenue at 88th Street
(212) 570-4751

13 A
Metropolitan Museum of Art
1000 5th Avenue at 82nd Street
(212) 535-7710

14 C
Shakespeare Garden, Central Park
79th Street and West Drive in the Park

15 C
Strawberry Fields, Central Park
Central Park West at 72nd Street

16 A
Frick Collection
1 East 70th Street
(212) 288-0700

17
Tavern on the Green, Central Park
Central Park at 67th Street
Open to the public for dining only

18 A
Abigail Adams Smith Museum
421 East 61st Street
(212) 838-6878

19 C
Trump Tower Trees
5th Avenue at 56th Street

20 C
Sculpture Garden at 590 Madison Ave.
Madison Ave. at 56th Street

21 A
Museum of Modern Art
11 West 53rd Street
(212) 708-9400

22 B
Paley Park
1 East 53rd Street

23 B
Greenacre Park
221 East 51st Street

24 C
Channel Gardens at Rockefeller Center
5th Avenue between 50th and 51st Streets

25 C
1251 Avenue of the Americas
Between 49 and 50th Streets

26 A
Japan Society
333 East 47th Street
(212) 832-1155

27 C
United Nations Garden
1st Avenue at 47th Street

28 A
Ford Foundation
320 East 43rd Street
(212) 573-5000

29 C
Bryant Park
Between 5th and 6th Avenues and
40th and 42nd Streets

30 A
Howard A. Rusk Institute of
Rehabilitation Medicine
400 East 34th Street
(212) 263-6058

31 A
General Theological Seminary
of the Episcopal Church
175 Ninth Avenue, between 20th
and 21st Streets
(212) 243-5150

32 C
Gramercy Park
Between 20th and 21st Streets,
between Lexington Avenue
& Irving Place

33 B
Jefferson Market Garden
Greenwich Avenue, between
6th Avenue and West 10th Street

34 B
9th Street Community Garden
and Park
9th Street and Avenue C

35 B
6 B–C Community Garden
624 East 6th Street

36 A
Merchant's House Museum
29 East 4th Street
(212) 777-1089

37 B
Brisas la Caribe
237 East 3rd Street

38 B
Liz Christie Garden
Bowery and Houston Street

39 C
Federal Plaza
Broadway between
Worth & Duane Streets

40 C
Winter Garden
at World Financial Center
West Street between Liberty
and Vesey Streets

41 C
Battery Park City
Between Battery Place,
State Street and the Hudson River

42 A
Bartow–Pell Mansion Museum
895 Shore Road, Pelham Bay Park,
Bronx
(718) 885-1461

43 A
Wave Hill
675 West 252nd Street, Riverdale,
Bronx
(718) 549-3200

44 A
New York Botanical Garden
200th Street and Southern Blvd., Bronx
(718) 817-8700

45 A
Queens Botanical Garden
43-50 Main Street, Flushing, Queens
(718) 886-3800

46 A
Isamu Noguchi Garden Museum
33-37 Vernon Blvd., Long Island City, Queens
(718) 545-8842

47 B
Carlton Garden
Carlton Street between Fulton
and Green Streets, Brooklyn

48 A
Brooklyn Botanic Garden
1000 Washington Avenue, Brooklyn
(718) 622-4433

49 A
Staten Island Botanical Garden
1000 Richmond Terrace, Staten Island
(718) 273-8200

50 A
Jacques Marchais Museum of Tibetan Art
338 Lighthouse Avenue, Staten Island
(718) 987-3500

51 A
Stephens–Prier House
at Historic Richmond Town
249 Center Street, Staten Island
(718) 351-1617

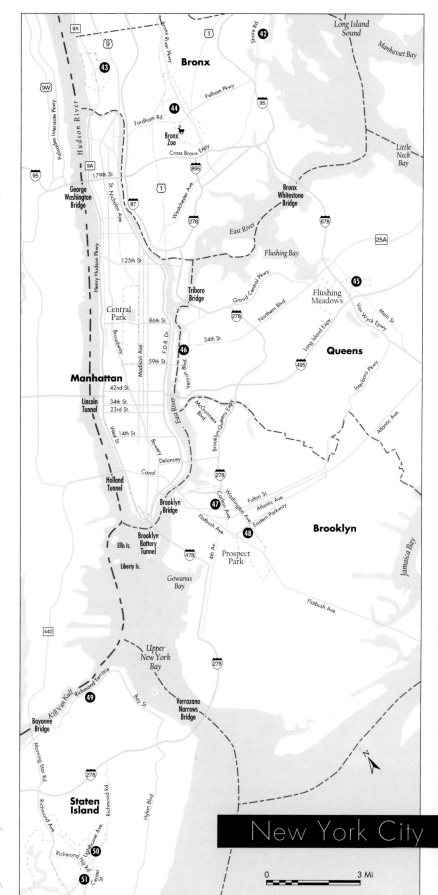

New York City

0   3 Mi

Arbor in the Peggy Rockefeller
Rose Garden, The New York
Botanical Garden

Author's Note

Early in 1990, Alessandro Albrizzi, landscape architect Bruce Kelly, and I started work on a book about the gardens of New York. Alessandro and I had just finished *The Gardens of Venice* and *The Gardens of Florence*, and Bruce thought it was time to put a sampling of the many wonderful gardens in the city of New York into one volume. No one had published a book like the one we envisioned, and we had high hopes for our collaboration. Alessandro, a Venetian who lived in New York most of the year, was a former Director of Photography for Réalités–Connaissance des Arts books, with work appearing in numerous publications in Europe and America. Bruce, a partner in the firm of Kelly/Varnell, Inc., had designed a number of imaginative and trend-setting gardens in the city. He directed us to public and private gardens that represented the great richness of material available, and Alessandro began to photograph. But then, sadly, Alessandro became too ill to continue and we put the book aside. Some of his photographs appear on these two pages in his memory.

MARY JANE POOL

Wisteria arbor, spiraea and
yew hedges in The Conser-
vatory Garden, Central Park

Strawberry Fields: A Garden of Peace

On the western edge of Central Park at 72nd Street, just across from the historic apartment building The Dakota, there is a tranquil stretch of garden. Conceived and funded by Yoko Ono as a memorial to her husband John Lennon, it is a tribute to his interest in international peace: 162 species of plant life represent each of the member states of the United Nations that gave a plant or an object to the garden. Landscape architect Bruce Kelly, an Olmsted scholar and one of the architects working on a master plan for Central Park, designed the serene landscape on 3½ acres. The vegetation is lush, with elegant trees, shrubs, and hundreds of strawberry plants.

Named for a song that Lennon composed for the Beatles, "Strawberry Fields Forever," the garden includes a large mosaic of his song title—"Imagine."

Photographs by Alessandro Albrizzi

Acknowledgments

So many have encouraged and assisted us in our preparations for this book. And it is amazing how many heads and hands it takes to publish such a volume. We wish to thank all the owners for allowing us to photograph and write about their gardens. And we also wish to thank the landscape designers and horticulturists who shared their knowledge about gardening in the city.

We greatly appreciate David Rockefeller writing the Foreword to our book. The Rockefeller family's dedication to public horticulture through the years has been a great gift to New York and is an example of how individuals can enhance the quality of city life.

Our thanks to Peter J. Johnson, Associate of David Rockefeller, and Barnett Shepherd, Executive Director of the Staten Island Historical Society, for their interest and help.

Some old friends, and new friends acquired along the way, have opened doors and given us their advice and support: Sharon Cogan-Beck, Clyde Cook, Miki Denhof, Joan Dunlop, Yves and Jacqueline Gonnet, Maurice and Georgine Goodman, Karen Gray, Richard V. Hare, Valerie Kalas, Margaret Kennedy, Diana Kline, Parker Ladd, Gregory Long, Frances Mastrota, Joyce Matz, Lisa Miller, Margaret Moore, Kathy Nutt, Michael Osheowitz, Betsy Barlow Rogers, Carole Rosenberg, Arnold Scaasi, Teri Slater, Kirkland Smith, Judy Struhl, Margaret Ternes, Rosa Toennies, George Trescher, Matthew Veralli, Thomas Versalla, Helen Weber, Jane Weissman, and Hiram Williams.

We are most grateful to the people who have given us permission to publish gardens belonging to their organizations, arranged for us to photograph, and answered our many questions: Peter Apgar, Andrea Bundonis, Mikki Carpenter, Joseph Carrillo, Nancy Chambers, Shelley Clark, Mark Danna, Mary Di Donato, Donna Faircloth, Lori Gold, Amy Hau, Elizabeth Hayes, Barbara Hayward, Robert Hyland, Susan Kaplan, Nora Keane, Karl Lauby, Sandra Manley, Amy Marth, Wendy Mijal, Ken Moss, Edgar Munhall, Bruce Parker, Chris Perez, Phillip A. Raspe, Jr., David Reese, Hilda Rodriguez, Nancy Ross, Avi Rubel, Karen Shnek, Anne Spira, Margaret Ann Tockarshewsky, Hisashi Yamada, and Yulianna Yevoushak.

Jay de Simone did early research on the subject for us, and the material she provided was most helpful in preparing the text.

It has been a joy working with a great publishing team at Harry N. Abrams, Inc. The enthusiasm of Paul Gottlieb, President and Editor-in-Chief, has inspired us. It was Margaret L. Kaplan, Senior Vice President and Executive Editor, who put photographer and writer together, guided us, and fashioned our work into this very special book. Designer Carol Robson interpreted our material beautifully and has given the book its great look and spirit. Assistant Editor Margaret Braver coordinated the early stages with grace and ease. Christine Edwards created the city map locating gardens open to the public.

Like a garden, a book idea takes on a life of its own as it grows. This particular book has taken a lot of tending, and we want to thank everyone for giving so very generously of their time and thought.

Mary Jane Pool
Betsy Pinover Schiff
New York, 1999

Photographer's Note

The beauty of the Brooklyn Botanic Garden first inspired my interest in gardens. At The New York Botanical Garden I learned to appreciate garden design and understand the immense amount of work required to create and maintain a distinguished garden. My association with these two great institutions led me to garden and landscape photography, and ultimately to this book.

My thanks to Mitchel Levitas, Tennyson Schad, and Roger Strauss III, for their invaluable advice; to Karen Fuller, Malcolm Spaull, and Michael Sokasits for their generous photography assistance; to Richard Kahn and Elaine Peterson, and to Ngaere Macray and David Seeler for their early encouragement of my garden photography; to Jay Maisel for helping me to see color through the camera; to LTI Photo for its excellent film processing and service.

Special thanks to my husband, Edward Schiff, for his constant support, his humor, and his love that keeps me focused on the beauty of life.

Betsy Pinover Schiff

Index

Note:
Pages in italics refer to illustrations.